THE PROPER AGGRESSIVENESS OF THE LORD'S SERVING ONES

WITNESS LEE

Living Stream Ministry
Anaheim, CA · www.lsm.org

First Edition, January 2009.

ISBN 978-0-7363-3797-7

Published by

Living Stream Ministry
2431 W. La Palma Ave., Anaheim, CA 92801 U.S.A.
P. O. Box 2121, Anaheim, CA 92814 U.S.A.

Printed by CPI Group (UK) Ltd, Croydon, CR0 4YY

09   10   11   12   13   14   15   /   9   8   7   6   5   4   3   2   1

CONTENTS

PREFACE

This book is composed of messages released by Brother Witness Lee to full-time serving ones on January 22-25, 1985 in Taipei, Taiwan.

CHAPTER ONE

LETTING NO ONE DESPISE YOUR YOUTH

First Timothy, 2 Timothy, and Titus, the three "T" books in the New Testament, are Epistles written by Paul to his two young co-workers, Timothy and Titus. The subject of 1 Timothy is God's economy concerning the church, the subject of 2 Timothy is an inoculation against the decline of the church, and the subject of Titus is the maintenance of order in the church. These are three aspects of one purpose, that is, to preserve the church as the proper expression of the Triune God.

TRUTH IN THE THREE "T" BOOKS

The three "T" books emphasize the truth. Hence, the word *truth* is used thirteen times (1 Tim. 2:4, 7; 3:15; 4:3; 6:5; 2 Tim 2:15, 18, 25; 3:7, 8; 4:4; Titus 1:1, 14). Four verses illustrate this emphasis on the truth.

Coming to the Full Knowledge of the Truth

First Timothy 2:4 says that God "desires all men to be saved and to come to the full knowledge of the truth." God desires all men to be saved. However, after salvation a man still needs to come to the full knowledge of the truth. *Truth* means "reality," and it denotes all the real things revealed in God's Word. In the New Testament there are many realities. For instance, the Word becoming flesh is a reality. The Word is God, and the flesh is fallen man. The Word becoming flesh means God coming to be a man in the likeness of the flesh of sin (Rom. 8:3). Furthermore, the Lord Jesus died on the cross to accomplish redemption. His death for the accomplishment of redemption is also a reality. Not only so, He resurrected; this is another reality. He ascended to the heavens, which is also a reality. Christ being life is a reality, His being the life-giving Spirit is a reality, and His being the resurrection is yet another reality.

To know the truth is to know the reality of the crucial points revealed in the New Testament. Instead of knowing doctrine, we must know the truth and obtain reality. The Word becoming flesh is a reality, the Lord's death and resurrection are a reality, and the Lord being the life-giving Spirit is a reality. Christ being life and resurrection are realities. As resurrection life, Christ becomes our sanctification, He becomes the power to sanctify us, and He becomes our overcoming life. These are also realities.

The Church as the Pillar and Base of the Truth

First Timothy 3:15-16 says, "The house of God, which is the church of the living God, the pillar and base of the truth...Great is the mystery of godliness: He who was manifested in the flesh." These two verses emphasize the church and speak of three main points concerning the church: the church is the house of the living God, the church is the pillar and base of the truth, and the church is the great mystery of godliness. These three points use different phrases to refer to the church, but they denote the same meaning. The house of the living God is the pillar and base of the truth, and the pillar and base of the truth is the great mystery of godliness, God manifested in the flesh.

Paul's sequence is right; he first speaks of the church as the house of the living God. God lives in this house. The kind of house a person lives in shows the kind of person he is. A house is the expression of the people who live in it. If an American family lives in a house for a month, it will have the expression of American family life; if a Japanese family lives in the same house, it will express the Japanese family life; similarly, if a Chinese family lives in a house, it will express the Chinese family life. This is the reason Paul says that the church is the house of the living God; the living God dwells in this house. This house manifests the truth, reality. This means that the living God, who manifests reality, dwells in this house and manifests Himself through this house. The living God is life, and He manifests life. The living God is sanctification, and He manifests sanctification. The living God is love, and He manifests love. Whatever God manifests is the truth, the reality of the divine things. This is the great mystery of godliness.

John 1:17 says, "The law was given through Moses; grace and reality came through Jesus Christ." When Jesus Christ came, God was expressed; God expressed is reality. God is manifested in the flesh. This refers not only to the incarnated Christ but also to the church as the enlargement of the incarnated Christ. Just as God was manifested in the flesh of Christ in the Gospels, God is manifested in the church, the enlargement of the incarnated Christ in the Epistles. The church as the house of the living God manifests the truth that it upholds. This is the great mystery of God manifested in the flesh.

Serving as Heralds of the Truth

According to 1 Timothy 2:7, Paul was appointed "a herald and an apostle..., a teacher of the Gentiles in faith and truth." Paul was a herald, an apostle, and a teacher in the sphere of faith and truth. Here *faith* refers to faith in Christ, and *truth* refers to the reality of all things in the economy of God as revealed in the New Testament. For instance, the Word becoming flesh, the death and resurrection of the Lord, and the Lord being the life-giving Spirit are all items of the truth, the reality in the economy of God. They are also the content of our faith, the items that we believe in.

Paul was sent not only to preach the gospel but also to teach people how to believe. This shows that we should not merely preach the gospel for people to be saved. After they are saved, we should teach them so that they understand what they have believed. This means that we should teach the realities, the truth, in the New Testament revelation as the content of the faith.

Cutting Straight the Word of the Truth

Second Timothy 2:15 says, "Be diligent to present yourself approved to God, an unashamed workman, cutting straight the word of the truth." *To cut straight* in Greek means "to divide." Just as a surgeon must know the human body so that he never randomly cuts a necessary part of the body, we must know the word of the truth so that when we expound the word of reality, the word of the truth, in the New Testament, we cut the word straight without any slant, curve, or distortion. When we expound the word of the truth incorrectly, we distort the word of the truth. Paul charged Timothy to learn to cut straight the word of the truth in the degraded situation of the church. In this way heresies and errors are avoided, and the factors of degradation are rooted out. This is a kind of inoculation.

THE RELATIONSHIP
BETWEEN FAITH, TRUTH, AND ECONOMY

The three "T" books also speak of faith, truth, and economy. Footnote 1 of 1 Timothy 1:1 in the Recovery Version shows the relationship between these three words. The faith is the contents of the complete gospel according to God's New Testament economy. This gospel is not an ordinary gospel; it is the complete gospel according to God's New Testament economy. The truth is the reality of the contents of the faith, and economy refers to the household administration of God. God is a God of economy. He has a dispensation, an arrangement, and a plan. God's economy is His plan. In eternity God had a plan, a dispensation, related to His household administration. There is a relationship between faith, truth, and economy: God's economy is His plan, faith is the contents of the gospel in God's plan, and truth is the reality of the contents of the faith.

NOT TEACHING DIFFERENTLY FROM GOD'S ECONOMY

Another emphasis in the three "T" books is Paul's charge to Timothy not to teach differently from God's economy. First Timothy 1:3-4 says, "I exhorted you, when I was going into Macedonia, to remain in Ephesus in order that you might charge certain ones not to teach different things nor to give heed to myths and unending genealogies, which produce questionings rather than God's economy, which is in faith." This portion shows that we should guard against and avoid teachings that differ from or distract from God's economy. However, we need to know God's economy, His arrangement, His plan. The primary matter is the gospel of God. The contents of the gospel of God is the faith, and the faith includes the reality of all the divine things. Therefore, what we preach must not differ from the words of reality in the divine things. This is our faith, this is the contents of the gospel, and this is the word of God's economy.

LETTING NO ONE DESPISE OUR YOUTH

In his Epistles Paul spoke many things to Timothy, but the most personal comment that he made to Timothy was, "Let no one despise your youth" (1 Tim. 4:12). This word, this charge, is inclusive in nature. It includes everything.

If a person receives teachings that are different from God's economy, he is naive. If he were not so, he would not agree with a speaking that is different from God's economy. If he agrees with a different teaching, he is not experienced and is still young. Therefore, we must learn to not let anyone despise our youth. Instead, we should be a pattern to the believers in word, in conduct, in love, in faith, and in purity (v. 12).

In Word

We should not let anyone despise our youth because of our words. We can discern whether or not a person is still a child by listening to how he speaks. Hence, in our serving the Lord we need to exercise to speak with weight and not frivolously. If our words are without weight, we are still young. This does not mean that we should speak with the sound and tone of an older man. Sounding like an older man is different from speaking with weight. We should not confuse these two things.

If we speak carelessly, we are not weighty and cannot be a pattern. In 1947 I was taking the lead in the church in Shanghai. One day while I was speaking with a few co-workers, a sister who loved the Lord ran into the room and exclaimed that there was a big hole in the ceiling upstairs. We were shocked and asked her how big the hole was. However, the more we inquired, the smaller the circle became. This shows that she was childish and young.

In Love

We also need to be a pattern in love. The object of a person's love usually is an indication of whether or not he is childish. A valuable ring is always displayed in a beautiful box. When a child sees the box, he may be attracted to the box and want the box instead of the ring. This shows that he is childish in his love. We need to mature in our love. Our love toward others should express maturity, not frivolity or childishness. In order to learn in these things, we should not read 1 and 2 Timothy and Titus too quickly. Rather, we should read them carefully and enter into each verse as if these Epistles were written to us personally.

In Purity

Even though Timothy was a young man, Paul charged him not to let others despise his youth in word, in conduct, in love, in faith, and in purity. Purity refers to being pure, without mixture, in motive and action. A person who is learning to serve the Lord should pray, "Lord, cause me not to give others any ground to say that I am childish, naive, and without learning in my conduct, actions, and words." This will take us a long time to learn.

In Fanning into Flame the Gift of God

"Let no one despise your youth" may also be applied to fanning into flame the gift of God, which is in us (2 Tim. 1:6). If the gift in us can be quickly fanned into flame but can only be sustained for five minutes, we are childish. We are also childish if we remain cold for half a year. We need to exercise so that our coldness lasts no longer than two minutes, but our being on fire lasts for twenty-five years. Some believers may say that this is extreme, but I do not think so. If we can continue to be on fire for ten or twenty years without getting cold, we are not childish; we have some maturity. There are saints in the church who are old yet still childish. They may be in their seventies, but they are still like a child. They are on fire today and cold tomorrow. They are "old children." Such believers can serve the Lord, but the effect of their service will not have a lasting impact. If we would like to have a lasting impact in our service, we must be experienced persons, not childish persons who fluctuate between hot and cold.

All the Charges Being Linked
to Letting "No One Despise Your Youth"

All the charges in 1 and 2 Timothy and Titus can be linked to the statement, "Let no one despise your youth." Paul charged Timothy to exhort an elderly man as a father and elderly women as mothers (1 Tim. 5:1-2). If we speak at length in a meeting, without discerning our audience or considering our age, we are childish. I once said that when a brother is appointed to be an elder, his wife might feel that she is the first lady. A young co-worker took these words and spoke in a meeting, saying, "Once a person becomes an elder, his wife immediately becomes the first lady." He then asked an elder whether his wife felt like she was a first lady. The way this young co-worker applied what I said indicated his lack of maturity.

It is all right for me as an elderly brother to speak such words, but it is not right for a young person to speak such things when he has no experience. At the most he could say, "Brother Lee said that everyone likes to be an elder and that after some brothers become elders, their wives regard themselves as first ladies." This is the most he should say. Saying anything further than this reveals his childishness. The young co-worker who spoke in this way left others with such a deep impression of his immaturity that it has not been forgotten even after many years.

When Timothy received Paul's Epistles, he might not have been more than thirty years of age. Even though he was young, Paul charged him to lay before the brothers what he had been taught (4:6). Paul also charged Timothy to appoint elders and to deal with accusations against the elders (5:19). These are serious matters. Not taking into account our age or the age of the ones whom we are speaking to will cause others to despise our youth. If we are older than those whom we are speaking to, our age gives us more ground to speak. However, if we are younger than those whom we are speaking to, we must remember this fact. When we pay attention to our age as well as the age of others, our speaking will be appropriate and no one will despise our youth.

CONCERNING THE CHARACTER OF THE LORD'S SERVING ONES

In summary, the three "T" books strongly emphasize the matter of character. These three books are involved with the character of a young person who serves the Lord. Paul admonished Timothy to practice the things that Paul had entrusted to him (1 Tim. 4:15). Being diligent is a matter related to character. Paul likened Timothy to a solider and to an athlete in a race (2 Tim. 2:3-5). Whether a person is a soldier or an athlete contending in the games, he must be trained in character. Paul used a soldier and an athlete as analogies to indicate that the Lord's serving ones must have proper character. Furthermore, Paul said to avoid vain babblings, which is related to character (1 Tim. 6:20; 2 Tim. 2:16). A person with poor character likes vain talk; once he starts a phone conversation, he cannot put the phone down. Therefore, by observing a person when he makes a phone call, we can gain an understanding of his character. The Chinese term for *character* is very meaningful. It is composed of two words: *xing* and *ge*. *Xing* refers to something inherent, and *ge* refers to something that is manifested; these two aspects form our character. That which is inward is innate, and that which is outward is cultivated. In 1953 while I was holding a training in Taiwan, I spoke of thirty items of character to the young trainees. The thirty items include: genuine, exact, strict, diligent, broad, fine, stable, patient, deep, pure, just, calm, single, corporate, open, affectionate, ardent, accommodating, strong, pliant, submissive, suffering, lowly, poor, steadfast, enduring, bearing, clear, magnanimous, and grave (see *Character*, published by Living Stream Ministry). I hope that especially the young saints will get into every character item.

CULTIVATING A PROPER CHARACTER

If a Chinese child is raised by Americans and grows up in an American society, he will acquire an American character.

Similarly, if an American child is raised by Chinese, he will have a Chinese character. This shows that character involves cultivation. According to my estimation, a person's character is determined thirty percent by nature and seventy percent by nurture. Whether or not we can do things appropriately and successfully depends entirely upon our character. Our ability is secondary; our character is the primary factor. May we all pay attention to this matter. On the one hand, we should not let anyone despise our youth; on the other hand, we must cultivate a proper character.

CHAPTER TWO

THE PURSUIT, CHARACTER, AND SERVICE OF THE FULL-TIMERS

NEEDING A SPIRIT OF PRAYER AND PAYING ATTENTION TO LIFE AND THE SPIRIT

A group of young saints recently consecrated themselves to serve full time. Seventy to eighty of them are from the church in Taipei, and the remaining one hundred twenty are from other places. The majority of these saints are between twenty-five and thirty-five years old, and they need to be trained in all aspects. However, the atmosphere of prayer for such a training is lacking. We cannot depend merely on a certain person to train them. We must increase our prayer, and we must have a spirit of prayer. These days are for prayer. We should even fast and pray.

Only the Lord is the Spirit, and only the Lord can train us. We should never think that we are establishing a theological seminary. Today's Christianity depends on theology, which is of no profit in accomplishing God's economy; hence, we cannot take the way of theology. Theology emphasizes neither life nor the Spirit, but we emphasize both life and the Spirit. The natural man tends to care for knowledge and organization, not for life and the Spirit. We cannot walk according to the tendency of the natural man; neither can we be without knowledge, because even though the writing of the Bible is according to the Spirit of life, the written word is through knowledge and is knowledge. If there were no written word, God could not put forth the revelation concerning life and concerning the Spirit. Therefore, we need to have knowledge. It is regrettable that Christianity leans toward knowledge and does not stress life and the Spirit. In the Lord's recovery we need to have proper knowledge of the Bible; however, we must not focus on knowledge. We must focus on life and the Spirit.

The brothers and sisters who desire to be in the training full time must have a new beginning with the Lord. This requires much prayer. How the training should be conducted requires our prayer. We should pray by ourself, when we come together in small numbers, and in the meetings. As a rule, we should pray unceasingly in the training meetings. We should pray and pray and pray. When our prayer is thorough, we will be clear concerning how to lead the training. Without sufficient prayer we will not know how the training should proceed. If we merely listen to messages to gain knowledge, we are taking a way that is not according to the Lord's leading. Hence, we should have a spirit of prayer.

DILIGENTLY STUDYING THE RECOVERY VERSION
AND THE LIFE-STUDY MESSAGES

The full-time trainees who are twenty-one years old should continue with their education and not consider full-time service until after they finish their college education. Every morning, from Monday to Friday, all the trainees must study the Recovery Version and the Life-studies. They should study the text, the footnotes, the Life-studies, and the cross references. How much they study the cross references depends on their time. However, they must read through and understand the text of the Recovery Version and study the footnotes. In addition, they must read and understand the Life-studies.

When we study, we first need to read the text according to the outlines. Once we understand the text, we can read the footnotes. After we understand the text and the footnotes, we should find the corresponding portion in the Life-study messages and go over the Life-studies with the text and the footnotes. I hope that the trainees will study five days every week, from eight o'clock in the morning to twelve noon. After studying for an hour, they can take a fifteen-minute break. It is better to study in groups of three or five. Saturdays should be set aside for service. If we are willing to practice this, after four years we will finish the entire New Testament.

CARING ONLY FOR THE BIBLE,
NOT THE CREEDS

We should pursue the truth by studying the Recovery Version and the Life-studies, but we should never consider this as our theology. The term *theology* is misleading. We have only the Bible; we do not have theology. The problems in Christianity began around the second or third century when the church fathers developed a theology from the Bible. In the Council of Nicaea in A.D. 325, the so-called Nicene Creed was instituted to determine the important doctrines and theology. On the one hand, the creed was written according to the New Testament, but not all of the books in the New Testament were recognized at the time. On the other hand, the creed was written according to the teachings of the church fathers. For some, the creed is now more authoritative than the Bible.

Even though some people advocate the creed and consider it to be according to the Bible, the creed is not as complete as the Bible. For example, Revelation, the last book of the Bible, speaks of the seven Spirits, but this is not in the Nicene creed. Moreover, the items in the Bible that are included in the creed are not covered in a detailed way. Furthermore, the Bible is different from all other books. Although scholars spend much effort to study the writing style of the Bible, rarely can one describe the style clearly. For example, it is difficult to define the style of writing in the Gospel of John. It differs from the style of writing commonly used by writers, and the topics, central line, emphases, and structure of the sections in this book are not immediately obvious to a reader. It is as if the points in this book are scattered like stars in the sky with here a little and there a little. Hence, we cannot systematize the Bible by applying systematic theology.

In 1983 I released a series of messages in Stuttgart, Germany, concerning the central view of the divine dispensing (see chapters 1 through 10 of *The Divine Dispensing of the Divine Trinity*). I have since studied the relationship between the Father and the Son, the Son and the Spirit, and the Spirit and the Father and found many important points. One point is that the Son comes with the Father. This is a crucial point.

However, the theology in Christianity does not emphasize the Son coming with the Father. Not even the creeds point out that when the Son was on the earth, the Father was with Him. Christian theology is even general in the way it says that the Father, the Son, and the Spirit coexist simultaneously. Unless a person studies this subject, he will not notice that the Son came with the Father.

Due to the incompleteness of the creeds, the British Brethren declared that they wanted the Bible, not the creeds. Later the Southern Baptist Church, one of the largest denominations in America, also declared that they wanted the Bible, not the creeds. The Church of Christ made the same declaration. More than sixty years ago, when we were raised up by the Lord in China, we also declared that we do not care for the creeds; we care only for the Bible. The creeds are not wrong, but because they are incomplete, they unavoidably cause people to err in their understanding.

In 1984 the Southern Baptist Church put out a publication with a list of all orthodox Christian groups, and we were included in this list. They also commented on several of our books, including *The Economy of God*. Their conclusion was that even though Witness Lee's exposition of the Bible may not be considered wrong, he adheres too closely to the lexical meaning of the Scriptures; hence, theologians who follow the creeds or base their beliefs on the various Councils find my exposition difficult to accept. After I read their conclusion, I said Hallelujah, because in America our slogan has always been "Return to the pure Word of God." The theology in various denominations in Christianity is not pure, but the truths in the Lord's recovery are entirely based on the Bible. Our interpretation of the Bible is based on the Bible, not on our own views.

Since the time of Brother Nee, the light that we have received has been progressing and increasing because we follow the Bible in our exposition. For example, before 1939, when Brother Nee spoke of our co-death with Christ, he stressed reckoning, based on the writings of A. B. Simpson, the founder of Christian and Missionary Alliance. One of Simpson's hymns says, "There's a little word that the Lord

has giv'n... / Let us reckon ourselves to be dead to sin"
(*Hymns,* #692). According to this hymn, the word that the
Lord has given us is *reckon*. Brother Nee translated this
hymn into Chinese. From 1938 to 1939 Brother Nee gave
the messages in *The Normal Christian Life* in which he
emphasized reckoning. However, after 1939 Brother Nee saw
that the fact of our co-death with Christ in Romans 6 can only
be experienced in the Spirit revealed in Romans 8. Therefore,
mere reckoning does not avail; we must be in the Spirit,
because the fact of our co-death with Christ is only in the
Spirit. In this matter Brother Nee had a great advancement.

Another example is concerning church practice. In 1934
Brother Nee conducted a Bible study with the co-workers
in Shanghai to study the church. The messages were published in *The Assembly Life.* After He completed the draft,
Brother Nee asked me to write a preface to the book. In this
book Brother Nee said that we did not have official apostles who establish churches; hence, no elders can be officially
appointed. Hence, at best we were unofficial apostles establishing unofficial churches and appointing unofficial elders.
Three years later, in 1937, Brother Nee gathered the co-
workers in Shanghai and gave messages that were later published as *The Normal Christian Church Life.* In these
messages he said that there are still apostles today and that
an apostle is one who is sent out by the Lord. Since there are
apostles, there are churches that are established by the apostles and elders who are appointed by them. This shows that
Brother Nee had a change in his understanding concerning
this matter. In 1948 several co-workers and I went to Brother
Nee's home in Foochow, and we stayed with him for some
time. While he was speaking with us, he said that in 1937 we
clearly saw the line of Antioch, but we neglected the line of
Jerusalem; however, we should stress the line of Jerusalem.
This does not mean that he had a different view, but it shows
that his view became more complete.

These examples show that we care only for the Bible, not
the creeds. If a person cares for the creeds, it is not possible
for him to change, and neither is it possible for him to
advance. In a few years we may see more than what we have

already seen. Our expounding of the Bible progresses and advances whenever we receive light. We cannot set up a creed to replace the Bible; this is evil before God. Although many denominations stress the creeds over the Bible, they cannot deny the fact that the Bible is a higher authority.

THE URGENT NEED TO KNOW THE BIBLE

From now on the full-time trainees must concentrate on studying the Bible. In the Lord's recovery we care only for the revelation of the Bible. We strongly disagree with the way of theological seminaries, which distorts the understanding of the Bible. Hence, the full-time trainees must realize their urgent need to know the Bible. But we will not set up a seminary or a Bible school to address this need. Instead, every trainee must spend half a day to study the Bible, until they are well versed in the Bible. Your foundation in the Bible is not solid; therefore, we need to rise up and catch up, putting in a good deal of effort to study the Bible.

It is difficult for the saints who are past sixty to study the Bible in this way. Nevertheless, it all depends on their effort. For example, I now study the Bible more than I did fifty years ago. However, you should not think that I have studied the Bible thoroughly, or that I have achieved success. I am still a student, and I am still studying. We study because we realize that our knowledge and experience fall short of the riches in the Bible. I therefore hope that the full-time serving ones will have a good beginning. You should not desire to be a spiritual giant or to become famous. You should serve in coordination with the brothers and sisters in your locality and spend half a day to study the Bible.

How you study is entirely up to you. You may take notes or underline the text. The only rule is that you set aside four hours every morning to study the Bible. I hope all the full-timers will accept this assignment. The saints who are part-time should also make an effort to study the Bible.

Furthermore, the brothers and sisters who serve full-time need to budget their time and make a schedule. Every morning from Monday to Friday, you must study the Bible for four hours and then serve in the afternoons and evenings and on Saturdays and Lord's Days. We have two major trainings every year. The summer training is around the time of the American Independence Day, and the winter training is around the Christmas and New Year holidays. While other people are enjoying their holidays, we are working and serving. This is what a full-timer should do.

Concerning your service, there is the work with children, the work on school campuses, and the gospel work in the community. We need further training in these areas. No matter which service we take part in, we must use four hours in the morning to study the Bible.

BUILDING UP OUR CHARACTER
FOR THE LORD'S SERVICE
BY HAVING NO OPINION

When we serve in coordination with the brothers in the church, we should keep the principle of having no opinion. From this time forward, we should begin to build up our character. Our nature is inherent, whereas our conduct is cultivated. Thirty percent of our character is innate, and seventy percent is cultivated. As we begin to serve the Lord, we should not only read the Bible and study the truth but also be trained in character for the Lord's service. The character needed for the Lord's service is higher than that for any other occupation.

The first and primary condition to cultivate a character for the Lord's service is to go against our disposition. If our disposition likes to talk, we should stand against our talking. We all share the common disposition of having opinions. We need to pay attention to this matter. After I was saved, I began to read the Bible in English and noticed that it differed from the Chinese translation of the Bible. I even wrote my older sister and said that the English translation was better than the Chinese translation of the Bible. In addition, I wrote down the verses that differed and their corrections based on the Bible in English and mailed the list to her. At the time, I enjoyed doing it. Later, as I had more learning, I felt that what I had done was childish and naive.

After many years I realized that the Chinese Union Version is a good translation that is even better than the King

James Version. The strength of the King James Version is in its good English structure. However, the King James Version was translated in the 1600s, and the manuscripts it is based on are less accurate than the manuscripts discovered later. In the 1800s a group of British and American Bible scholars formed a committee to revise the King James Version, but they had different views on many points, including whether to use the name *Jehovah*. The British scholars, who advocated using *Lord,* published the Revised Standard Version. While the American scholars, who advocated using *Jehovah,* published the American Standard Version. This version was completed in 1901.

Western missionaries translated the Old and New Testaments into Chinese using the Revised Version and the manuscripts in the Hebrew and Greek languages. This translation is called the Chinese Union Version and was published in 1919. It is widely used by Christians in China and is one of the best translations into Chinese. The language is of a high standard, and it is based on manuscripts that are more accurate than those used for the King James Version.

You will not encounter the difficulties that I encountered as a new believer when you study the Bible, because we have been studying the truth for the past sixty years. Hence, you will not waste your time. As we learn the Bible, we should have no opinion. I hope that we build up a character to learn without opinions. We should never criticize a version of the Bible as being wrong, even though our translation of the Bible is based on years of experience as well as the studies of many scholars throughout the generations.

It took us a significant amount of time to translate the Recovery Version into English, and we are still revising it. Several full-time brothers in America are currently comparing the Recovery Version with the Greek text with the view of publishing a revised edition. When we were working on the Recovery Version, we consulted many translations and the best reference books. The Recovery Version is not something produced from our imagination, neither was it done by merely consulting a Greek dictionary and a few reference books. Rather, we took the original text as our basis, and then considered the strengths of different versions. After careful evaluation and consideration, we made our decisions.

Even more time and effort were spent to write the footnotes. We are standing on the shoulders of all the orthodox biblical scholars over the past nineteen centuries. We collected and consulted writings from the time of the church fathers until the present day. None of our work was done hastily. Therefore, we should not criticize the footnotes that differ from our concept; rather, we should learn from them. We should not have any opinions, because opinions damage a person greatly.

Likewise, when we learn to serve in the different localities, we should not disapprove if there is something in the coordination that differs from our view. Our disapproval shows that we are naive. In order to build up our character for the Lord's service, we must learn to have no opinions. When we study the truth, we should be diligent without having any opinions, and when we serve the Lord, we should labor diligently without any opinions. We should always learn to work without opinions. If we are vacuuming a room, we should do it thoroughly and not criticize, which is to express an opinion. I hope that as we serve, we will have no opinions. We will know only to be diligent and to labor by doing more and learning more. We should all build up such a character.

Then we will become useful persons. In the future many of us will be able to give messages according to the Bible. The way to give a message that will stir up people's interest is to speak according to the Bible, that is, to speak by expounding the Bible. This is the most powerful way to speak. There is no book that can meet the standard of the Bible. Therefore, the best way to give a message is to expound the Bible, but this requires a thorough knowledge of the Bible. Gaining such knowledge takes extensive training. Hence, we must spend the next four years to lay a good foundation in the New Testament. We can begin with Paul's fourteen Epistles and read them in sequence, starting from Romans. After the fourteen Epistles, we can read the Gospels, Acts, and James through Revelation.

HELPING THE SMALL GROUPS

Another burden of the training, which will be brought up

in subsequent fellowship, is that every full-timer should help a small group. This does not mean we will lead the small groups; we will help them. On the one hand, I am concerned that the full-timers may become proud upon hearing that they are qualified, designated, and commissioned to help the small groups. On the other hand, the brothers and sisters in the small groups may say, "Didn't Brother Lee say that there are no responsible ones or leading ones in the small groups? Why then does he ask trainees to help us?" We need to see that in order to avoid doing things in a natural way in the small groups, the small groups need the help. In order to help the small groups, the trainees need to know the complications related to a small group.

In the Lord's recovery our practices are not mechanical or organizational; they are organic. Hence, it is wrong for the full-time brothers and sisters to help the small groups in an organizational way. Our help must be organic. It is not easy to know what is organic and what is organizational. In the training we will be perfected to help the small groups, after which we will be assigned to a small group. If our attitude is that we know how to help people and, hence, we are the coach, what we do will become organizational. We should have the attitude of being a brother or a sister, who is a member of the Body, meeting together with our brothers and sisters in a small group. We should not feel that we are there to help others and that the other members must receive our help.

We must be organic in the small group. Even though this is not easy, if we learn, every small group will be revived. For example, in a small group gathering, if a person suddenly brings food and invites everybody for a feast, should we join them? Or should we give a message telling them that a small group meeting should not be worldly? What is the best way to handle the situation? A brother may say that we need to turn to our spirit, eat in spirit, and bring everyone into Christ through eating. This may sound good, but it is not so easy to carry out. One way to handle the situation is to not do anything. We can simply eat with them, not expecting to do anything, because there is not much we can do under that kind of atmosphere. Therefore, the best way is to not do anything and to not say anything. Just eat with them.

After we finish eating, we should not look for an opportunity to correct them. Even if we would tell them that material things are a type of spiritual things, we should speak in a careful way, because if we are not careful in our speaking, it can be insinuating. The most appropriate way is to say something uplifting when we are invited to speak. We should speak Christ but not say anything related to eating. Mentioning the food is like exposing a scar. We must avoid speaking in this way. We should only speak something inspiring so that they may get the benefit. Perhaps we will not have the opportunity to help them on that day, or even on the second or third visit. If we can endure until the fourth meeting, perhaps by then we will know how to work in a small group.

The time will come when the Holy Spirit will prepare an environment to render help in a spontaneous way. Therefore, as we go out to help people, we should not seek to be quick, nor should we focus on quick success. It may be that we visit them for half a year, and we still cannot help them. Please remember that there is no wasted effort. As long as we are going, this is better than not going.

We should realize that they are not completely without feeling concerning eating the feast. There is some feeling in them, but how deep and how strong their feeling is depends on how much weight we have before the Lord. If the apostle Paul were there, they would have a heavy feeling. Therefore, it is likely that due to our presence, they will begin to feel something. Therefore, we do not need to do something immediately. We simply need to go again and again. I believe that the Holy Spirit will give us an opportunity, and our effort will not be wasted. To learn to not do anything is an important lesson. We are doing a spiritual work, and this is the secret. May we all have this exercise. Gradually, the small groups will be delivered from the natural way of doing things, and people will receive the supply of life from us.

CHAPTER THREE

THE LEARNING NEEDED
FOR THE SMALL GROUP MEETINGS

TURNING FROM LARGER MEETINGS
TO SMALL GROUP MEETINGS

The church is making a turn in its practice from corporate meetings involving all the saints to meetings in small groups. Corporate meetings involving all the saints are suitable in a small locality with about one hundred saints, because they can meet the needs of the saints. But when the number in the meetings increases, the needs of the saints who are at different levels will be overlooked in meetings that involve all the saints. Even though human beings tend to be gregarious, we live in households as the basic unit; we do not live in groups. The strength of a country and the stability of its society depend on the household as its basic unit. If the household unit is destroyed, a society becomes corrupted and the country is weakened.

Breaking Bread and Praying from House to House

The principle is the same with the church. In the church the household is the basic unit. On the day of Pentecost three thousand people were saved (Acts 2:41). These new believers gathered in the temple and broke bread and prayed from house to house (vv. 42, 46). They needed to gather together so that the apostles could teach them. However, this was not enough; there was still the need for the believers to break bread and have mutual fellowship and prayer in their homes, that is, from house to house. By the end of chapter 5 the small gatherings in the homes were not only for the breaking of bread and prayer but also for announcing the gospel of Jesus as the Christ (v. 42). They announced the Lord Jesus as the gospel from house to house. Chapter 20 reveals that during

Paul's three years in Ephesus, he declared the counsel of God to the Ephesians publicly and also entreated and admonished them from house to house (vv. 18-20, 31).

Based on these verses, after a local church increases, it must take the household unit as its base. We have neglected this for the past twenty years and have suffered a great loss. On the one hand, we have preached the gospel, baptized people, and led many to salvation, but on the other hand, not many of these have remained. The root cause is that we neglected the matter of the household as a unit. Church history and world history show that the existence of any large group is based on small units within the group. Therefore, the church in Taipei must have a great turn from corporate meetings involving all the saints to small groups. Other than having a need for an administrative government, the small group should function according to all the other aspects of a local church.

Taking Care of Four Matters—
Teaching, Shepherding, Care, and Support

Whether a local church is strong or weak depends on how the church takes care of teaching, shepherding, caring for, and supporting the saints. If a local church takes care of these four matters, it will be healthy. How can the elders take care of these four items in a large local church? For example, thirty elders would not be able to take care of these four matters in the church in Taipei, where there are three thousand people who meet regularly. At most, the elders could gather the saints into meetings and give them messages. But this only takes care of teaching, and even this teaching cannot be thorough. The elders would be unable to shepherd, care for, and support all the saints. Because we did not take care of these matters in the past, all the ones saved through us either died or were adopted by others. If we want our children to grow up in the homes, there should be shepherding, care, and support at home.

Having Many Small Groups
but Still Being One Church with One Eldership

We are raising up the small groups so that we can make

up the lack in shepherding, care, and support. The co-workers and elders in Taipei must realize that the building up of the church is entirely dependent on the small groups. In the small groups there should be teaching, shepherding, care, and support. This does not mean that there is absolutely no administration or management in the small groups, but the need for this is not great. The life pulse of a small group is in teaching, shepherding, care, and support. We can no longer follow our old ways; in other words, we have changed our administrative system. However, this does not mean that we do not need elders; neither does it mean that every home should be regarded as a church. It is wrong to say that every home is a church.

Someone said that as long as there are a few believers meeting in a home, that home is a church. He spoke this based on Paul's word in the Epistles concerning the church in a person's house (cf. Rom. 16:5; 1 Cor. 16:19; Col. 4:15; Philem. 2). But this is a mistaken view. The believers in Jerusalem met from house to house, but Acts 8:1 refers to "the church which was in Jerusalem." According to the original Greek, *church* here is singular, implying one church in one locality. There were many home meetings in Jerusalem, but they were one church.

According to the record in Acts, there was only one group of elders in the church in Jerusalem. Hence, Barnabas and Paul handed the material offering to the elders in the church in Jerusalem (11:30). In chapter 15 when a problem arose in the churches, Paul and Barnabas went to Jerusalem to see the elders and the apostles (v. 2). This proves that a large church with thousands of believers meeting in numerous homes is still one church. In this way, the oneness of the Body of Christ in each locality is kept.

The Practice of the Church Life and
the Building Up of the Church
Being Carried Out in the Small Groups

Whereas the administration and the management of a church are with the eldership, the practice of the church life and the building up of the church are carried out in the small groups. Hence, there is the need for every group to function and take care of the responsibility of teaching, shepherding, care, and support. If we try to take care of these four matters in the big meetings, they will never be accomplished. For example, even though many women work and send their children to a daycare center, the center cannot raise the children. The mothers still have to fulfill their responsibility of raising their children at home.

In the Bible there is a model of the church in Jerusalem, which was a large church. The management and administration of the church in Jerusalem was under one eldership, but the shepherding and building up of the church life were carried out in the homes. The church in Taipei is also a large local church. The responsibility of teaching, shepherding, care, and support must be transferred to the groups and borne by the groups. This can be compared to a country needing families to raise its young citizens. As long as every family does a good job, the country will be strong and prosperous. Therefore, if a local church can take good care of teaching, shepherding, care, and support, it will grow in life and be full of vigor. It will also be easy for the church to be built up. I hope that the elders in the localities, especially those from large localities, will realize that this is the time for the church life in the Lord's recovery to take a big turn. We are turning from shepherding in large meetings to teaching, shepherding, care, and support in small groups.

THE PURSUIT OF THE FULL-TIMERS

The full-timers who are serving the Lord should set aside four hours every morning, from Monday to Friday, to have a good foundation in the truth. Christianity relies on its theology, but we rely on every saint knowing the Bible. Knowledge of the Bible is the foundation of our service. Hence, all the full-timers must make a resolution to spend four hours to study every day. I hope that all the leading ones and co-workers will help the trainees study without distractions. Furthermore, I would ask the elders and co-workers to supervise the young full-timers to make sure that they spend four hours on the Lord's Word. We should try our best to assist them to learn to use their time appropriately.

THE SERVICE OF THE FULL-TIMERS—
HELPING THE SMALL GROUPS

Besides getting into the Word, the full-timers should serve in the small groups. This is a huge task. There are many details involved, because there should be teaching, shepherding, care, and support in the small groups. There are countless lessons for us to learn regarding these four matters.

Not Putting on Airs

Suppose we go to a small group and have the attitude that since we are full-time serving ones who study the Bible every day, our knowledge of the Bible is superior. Gradually, those attending the group meetings will stop coming. Even if they do not say anything openly, they will be stumbled by our attitude. Our putting on airs will scatter the whole flock of sheep.

Twenty years ago I discovered that of the twenty thousand saints in the church in Taipei, only three or four thousand actually came to the meetings. There was a large number of absentees. Hence, I suggested that the elders use a scientific method to find out why these saints do not come to the meetings. They were asked to analyze whether the saints were absent because they were poor and needed to work for their living, because they were sick, or because of something else. Regrettably, this was never carried out. There are many reasons that the saints do not come to the meetings. One reason is that the leading ones put on airs. The moment that we consider ourselves to be higher than others, the saints stop coming to the meetings. For this reason, there are no responsible or leading ones in our arrangement of the small groups. The full-timers should never consider themselves to be somebody and think that since they are trained, since they study the Bible diligently, and since they have passed some examinations, they are full-time co-workers. Such a consideration will do them much harm. Those who put on this kind of "uniform" will cause great harm.

When full-timers go to a small group, they should put off all such uniforms. This is not an easy thing to do, because sometimes when you put off a uniform, others try to put it back on you. At any rate, when you go to a small group meeting, you should never go with a special status; you should realize that you are simply a brother or sister. This is good enough. We should not even adopt the term that we are "helpers," because no matter what term we use, it will mistakenly be used as a title. This is truly not good.

Having No Status

In the group meetings we should remember that we have no status. We are only brothers and sisters. This is our common status. A full-timer may consider that since he is serving the Lord, he must do a good job even if others do not. Some saints have the concept that since the full-timers are supported by the offerings of the saints, the full-timers should labor more than other saints.

I once heard a saint say, "What do the full-timers do? Most saints go to work every day to make a living, but the full-timers are carefree because the church supports them. Is it not right for them to take care of the service in the church?" Many saints have heard comments similar to this. Some working saints think that since they are not full-timers, they do not need to do much. They want the full-timers to do everything. This is not proper, just as it is not proper for full-timers to consider themselves more than simply brothers and sisters.

Arriving Early, Fellowshipping Spontaneously, and Having No Opinions

When you go to a group meeting, you must be early. For example, if a group meeting is at seven-thirty in the evening, you should not arrive after seven-thirty. When you arrive early, you can have fellowship with the host family or care for their children. You are serving the Lord and should never arrive late. If you arrive late, you cannot do much, but if you arrive early, you can do much. When you arrive early, you should not sit down and be glued to a chair. You may ask the saints if there is anything you could do to help. You can help with the setting up of chairs. However, when you set up the chairs, you should not have any opinions. All of us have the same problem. When we do nothing, we have no opinions, but once we begin to do something, our opinions surface. You might suggest that the chairs should be set up this way or that way. If you do this, the host will be offended and think that you are giving him commands. Even if the host turns the chairs upside down, you should learn to follow him without any opinion. You should simply follow what he does; you should not have any opinions, and neither should you mention anything, inquire about anything, or promote anything.

If no one else is present when the meeting is supposed to begin, you should not say, "Why is no one here?" You should never be a busybody. In the group meetings you will discover that you have many defects. This can be likened to a daughter who is learning from her mother how to cook. Even though the daughter has not yet learned to cook, she will often try to instruct her mother to do this or that. Actually, if the daughter would speak less and observe more, she would learn how to cook.

Being Prudent and Wise

If we are willing to receive this fellowship, we will grow after being in a group meeting for six months. When we enter a home, we may find a baby crawling on the floor, and we can care for him. Eventually, we will learn to fellowship with the young and with the older saints. However, if we enter into a home, and the husband has not returned from work, the wife is in the kitchen, and the baby is crawling on the floor, and we murmur that no one is present, the host family will be cold toward us. A serving one of the Lord needs to be prudent. We should play with the baby and even talk with him, or we can help the wife in the kitchen.

If we help with the baby or in the kitchen, this will warm the mother's heart. Then later in the meeting, the mother will listen to what we say. If damaging words come out of our mouth when we enter the home, we should not expect the mother to listen to us in the meeting.

Maintaining Fellowship
with the Lord in the Spirit

Whether we fellowship with others or do things, we must

constantly fellowship with the Lord in prayer. We can ask the Lord to give us something appropriate to say. We should not play politics when we speak with others; rather, we should live in the spirit and fellowship with the Lord. The Lord will give us suitable words in a timely manner. Some saints do not know how to speak with others. We all need to learn.

When we join a small group, we should not speak too much; neither should we be silent. However, it is not so easy to be balanced. Let us consider the previous example. When we see a baby crawling on the floor, we should not speak too much lest we express our opinions, but we should not sit silently either. It is not so easy to offer our portion to supply others in a way that can be received by others. Therefore, I would exhort all the brothers and sisters who are serving full time to learn earnestly. This is because we are all beginners, and people need time to trust in us. We may have knowledge, but no one knows this. Thus, it can be difficult for others to accept our speaking right away. If we are willing to learn these things, the saints will be happy to open their homes to us. Hence, we must receive the help from the training and exercise diligently.

Not Organizational but Organic

If the saints in a group meeting sit silently, we should learn to be patient and not do anything. Even if it is difficult to endure the silence, we should never start anything; we should simply be in the meeting.

In 1937 I was invited to speak concerning the book of Hebrews at a training for preachers. At that time, they also invited me to join their meetings in various places. One time I asked, "When does your morning meeting begin?" They said, "We ask the saints to meet in the morning, but we do not say what time. All of our believers tend to trickle in one by one from nearby villages. We wait until they all arrive, and then we sound a bell and begin the meeting." Afterward I went to join one of their morning meetings. It was one-thirty in the afternoon by the time everyone sat down. When I asked, "Why do these Western missionaries not teach people to keep the time?" I learned that these Western missionaries did not want to touch the matter of meeting on time because this would inhibit the believers from wanting to come to the meeting. In this matter I learned a lesson.

We are being trained to be on time, but when we go out to serve, we should always remember that the brothers and sisters have not been trained. We may be in a hurry and want to begin a meeting on time, but they are used to arriving late. This is a test to us. If we fail the test, the group meeting will fail.

Some may ask how can there be a meeting if everyone is late. We should be patient. Perhaps after six months, we can encourage the saints not to be late. We should wait until we are able to render this type of help. When the saints know us, they will appreciate the help. Therefore, we must not do anything in the way of organization; we must be organic.

RECEIVING A FOUNDATION

We thank the Lord and rejoice to see that the majority of the full-time trainees are under thirty-five years of age. Hence, we must learn earnestly. This one or two years of training is a foundation for the trainees. It will be a great help when they serve the Lord in the future.

Praying Daily for Wisdom

In 1932 I had been saved for seven years, and I was used by the Lord to establish a small church in my hometown. Later the Lord compelled me to give up my job and serve full time. Eventually, the Lord brought me to Shanghai. At that time I learned from Solomon to pray, "Lord, give me wisdom, that I may know how to go out and come in before Your people" (cf. 2 Chron. 1:10). I prayed in this way for several years. As I look back, I feel that the Lord has heard my prayer. The trainees should also pray, "Lord, I am still young and only beginning to learn to serve You. Give me wisdom so that I may know how to go out and come in before Your people."

Studying Seriously the Three "T" Books

In 1 Timothy 3:15 Paul says, "If I delay, I write that you may know how one ought to conduct himself in the house of

God." *How to conduct oneself in the house of God* means "how to behave and act in God's house." The three books of 1 Timothy, 2 Timothy, and Titus clearly state how a serving one should conduct himself and how he should cultivate his character. The trainees need to study these books diligently.

There are several terms in these books that are worthy of attention: *turning away* (1 Tim. 6:20), *avoid* (2 Tim. 2:16; Titus 3:9), and *flee* (1 Tim. 6:11; 2 Tim. 2:22). We should study what things to turn away from, what things to avoid, and what things to flee from. In addition, we should depart from unrighteousness (v. 19), refuse a factious man (Titus 3:10), and refuse profane and old-womanish myths (1 Tim. 4:7). We should find and study such terms in these books. Then we will know which things to turn away from, which things to avoid, which things to depart from, and which things to refuse. When we flee, we must do it quickly. When we avoid something, we must stay a good distance from it. When we turn away, we must behave as if we were facing an oncoming car. If we do not turn away, we will be in a car accident. All of us should have the thoughts of fleeing, avoiding, and turning away.

These books also speak of the conscience: a pure conscience (3:9; 2 Tim. 1:3) and a good conscience (1 Tim. 1:5, 19). They speak of holding the mystery of the faith in a pure conscience (3:9), which mystery is God's economy. We see from the Scriptures that the mystery of God is Christ (Col. 2:2), and the mystery of Christ is the church (Eph. 3:4). We need to have a pure conscience to hold the mystery of the faith. Our conscience is an indication of whether we are holding the mystery of the faith; hence, we need to conduct ourselves in order to have a pure conscience. Some people thrust their faith and conscience away and become shipwrecked regarding the faith (1 Tim. 1:19). All these are related to cultivating our character. We must study these books diligently.

Furthermore, we should not merely learn the truth and grow in life; we must also learn how to serve and how to be wise. Such matters cannot be learned in one or two days. If it requires one or two years to learn how to play basketball, it is even more necessary to practice in the matter of serving the Lord.

CHAPTER FOUR

THE PRACTICE OF FELLOWSHIP
IN THE SMALL GROUPS

Prayer: Lord, we truly need Your mercy and Your grace. We do not know what to do or how to go on, so we look to You to lead us. As we are fellowshipping, cause us to touch Your leading and Your heart's desire. We are not clear concerning how to go on in the bread-breaking meeting, the prayer meeting, and the gatherings in the small groups. Show us Your way so that we may go on faithfully to learn and practice. Lord, cleanse us again, and anoint us bountifully with Your rich anointing. Bless our fellowship, and bless us in our practice. Lord, fight for us against the attacks and troubles from the enemy, especially His attacks on our bodies. Bind the evil one, and rebuke the demons. We reject all the demons in Your victorious name. Amen.

FELLOWSHIP IN THE SMALL GROUPS
BEING ALL-INCLUSIVE IN NATURE

We will study how to have a small group gathering. In a small group gathering we can break bread, pray, and fellowship. In function the small group meeting covers all the aspects of the church life. In the small groups there can be teaching, which is related to the aspect of the truth; there can be shepherding, which is related to the aspect of life; and there can also be care and support, which are related to the aspect of practical living. In addition, in the small groups we can also preach the gospel. If a church can be thorough in its teaching of the truth, in its shepherding in life, and in its care and support in practical living, then it can be considered as being established. If a church as large as the church in Taipei relies only on the leading by the elders in large corporate meetings, the church will not be able to function in these aspects. The church must be divided into small groups for the teaching of the saints. It is inappropriate to teach in the Lord's table meeting, the prayer meeting, or the gospel meeting; teaching involves fellowship. Teaching, shepherding, care, and support involve fellowship. Hence, fellowship is all-inclusive and multi-purposed in nature; it is complete in nature. For this reason, meetings involving fellowship are the most difficult.

The Bible Being Necessary
for Teaching and Shepherding

Teaching cannot be separated from the truth in the Bible. Moreover, shepherding and teaching are a twofold cord that is actually one. In Ephesians 4:11 shepherds and teachers are the same group of people. In order to shepherd people, one must know how to teach, and in order to teach effectively, one must be a shepherd. Therefore, when shepherding and teaching, as two cords of a rope, are combined, there is strength. For this reason, it is necessary to use the Bible when we fellowship in the small groups; otherwise, we can neither teach nor shepherd. When teaching and shepherding are carried out properly, there will be care and support. Hence, the key is how to use the Bible when we fellowship in a small group.

The Best Materials Being
the Recovery Version and the Life-study Messages

In the fellowship meeting of the small groups we can use the Recovery Version and the Life-study messages as materials. Life is the line, the focus, and the content of the Life-study messages. The Bible is a book of life, the history of the Bible supports the line of life, and the characters in the Bible are illustrations of life. Everything in the Bible centers on life. Bible scholars throughout the centuries have expounded the Bible from the aspect of knowledge, from the aspect of people, from the aspect of history, and from the aspect of proverbs or teachings. The focus of every exposition is different. I have read many books of exposition, but I have not found one that takes life as its center. Because of the Lord's unveiling, I understood that the expounding of the Bible should take life as its focus and its line. Hence, this was my focus in my writing the Life-studies.

I began to use the term *life-study* in 1950. After we finished the first formal training in 1953 in Taiwan, I felt that we should have a life-study of the Bible. Therefore, beginning from 1954 I conducted the life-study of the Bible for about one year, and it was blessed by the Lord. We did a rough study of the Old Testament, but we were more detailed when we came to the New Testament. Thus, *life-study* became an official term among us; I also wrote the outlines of the life-studies.

From 1974 I began to lead a formal life-study training in America. So far, we have spent eleven years writing the *Life-study of the New Testament,* taking life as the focus and the line. Since this is an exposition of the Bible, we paid attention to the readers' understanding of the Bible. If we do not understand the words when we read the Bible, we can stay only on the surface, and it will be difficult for us to get into the depths. It is not so easy to understand the words in the Bible, because the Bible contains a vast number of special terms. Furthermore, the Bible uses unique and profound words; hence, they are not so easy to explain.

For decades I have spent my time and energy studying the Bible, consulting the writings of many well-known authors of the past centuries. Hence, I feel assured that I am able to provide a proper explanation of important phrases and words, especially in the New Testament. Hence, many footnotes of the New Testament are expository in nature. For instance, in Romans 1:2 there is a footnote for the word *holy*. Because the word *holy* is an important term in the Bible, I provided a thorough explanation. There are quite a number of footnotes like this. This kind of exposition is not for those who read the Bible casually but for those who desire to devote themselves to studying the Bible.

When we fellowship in a small group, we must use the Bible. However, when we use the Bible, it is best to use the text and the Life-study messages, rather than focusing on the footnotes or the cross references. Suppose we are reading the book of Romans. Initially, the saints may be interested in reading it, but if we try to explain the word *holy* in great detail, they may not understand it. Hence, we must understand that the text of the Recovery Version is the starting point for everyone, because some of the footnotes are not easy to understand. If we desire to serve the Lord full time, we must labor in the Bible. This is a requirement that cannot be evaded. However, when we go to a small group meeting, we should not use it to show off our knowledge.

THE PRACTICE OF FELLOWSHIP IN A SMALL GROUP

According to our present situation there is an urgent need for the light of the truth and the supply of life in the small groups; there is not much need for in-depth explanation. In our practice of the small groups, we need to have the light of the truth and the supply of life.

When we come to a small group meeting, there should not be any formality. The meeting can begin in any way. If the chair that you sit on is not comfortable, you can switch to a little stool. In a small group there is no need for polite talk or religious rituals and methods. When we come together, we should greet one another spontaneously and have a spirit of mutual concern, mutual teaching, and mutual care. We may say, "Thank the Lord, we have two more saints today than the last time." Another saint may say, "Yes, I really thank the Lord. Last time I came and tasted the sweetness of fellowship among the saints, so I am here again today." Then a more experienced saint may say, "Thank the Lord, our fellowship last time was really sweet," and he may continue with a prayer: "Lord, we thank You that this brother came last week and was touched and graced by You." In this way, spontaneously everyone will enter into prayer. Perhaps the brother who was graced by the Lord would follow in prayer and say that he received much help last time from reading a portion from Romans. This is a good opportunity to enter into the truth of the Bible according to his need.

To pursue the truth in fellowship during a small group meeting, we can use the Recovery Version as much as it is needed. The purpose of reading the Recovery Version is to help the saints understand the Bible, see light in the truth, and receive the supply of life. This depends on our labor in the Word. Hence, before the meeting we must read through the portion of the Scriptures that will be covered that day with the related footnotes and Life-study messages.

We can practice with Romans 1:1-4. In the meeting we can read the outline for this portion and then read the text. In the small group there may be time to read only four verses, but in our preparation we should prepare more verses. We do not need to read the footnotes, nor do we need to recite the verses. We only need to remember the thought in the verses. After reading the verses, some saints can speak the content of the verses. The more experienced saints can add a little explanation of the verses. Then there can be prayer related to the content of the verses: "Lord, we truly thank You. You are the subject of the gospel. The gospel is not concerning heaven or hell but concerning You. According to the flesh, You are the Son of Man, and indeed You are a man. According to the Spirit of holiness, You resurrected from the dead and were designated the Son of God. Hence, You are the Son of God. You are God."

The footnotes are for us to be equipped. Hence, we need to study the footnotes thoroughly. If someone in the small group meeting asks about the meaning of the Spirit of holiness, we can explain, but not in the way of a study. We can also say that if the saints want to know more, they can get a copy of the Recovery Version and study it.

In order to use the Life-study messages, we must prepare before the meeting so that we know which points need to be stressed and which points do not. For example, Message 2 of the *Life-study of Romans* is on the gospel of God. Suppose the first paragraph is read in the meeting. When you get to the portion that says, "The Christ in the four Gospels was among the disciples; the Christ in Romans is within us," we should take the opportunity to speak three or five sentences to stress this point. We may say, "After Christ died and resurrected, He became the life-giving Spirit who dwells in our spirit." Or we can select a different portion from the message that concerns

Christ and read it together to emphasize life and not truth. In this case we may say to the others, "The book of Romans shows that the Lord Jesus today is not the same as He was with Peter, James, and John. Today He has passed through death and resurrection and has become the life-giving Spirit to dwell in us and to be our life practically. We have the same life and the same living with Him." Then all the saints can fellowship based on the portion of the message that was read.

After the fellowship we can give a three to five sentence summary, such as, "Paul's word in this portion is a crystallized speaking. It shows that our precious Lord Jesus is a man in the flesh. He is also God with divinity. He went through human living, died, resurrected, and became the life-giving Spirit to dwell in us. We hope that after this fellowship we all will live in Him every day, taking Him as our life, having fellowship with Him daily, and living Him out." All those in attendance will never forget this kind of summary.

EVERYONE BEING A PROPHET AND A TEACHER AND EVERYONE FUNCTIONING

All the co-workers and elders should participate in the small groups and help the group meetings. Especially since we are at the initial stage of the work, we must have a strong beginning. Furthermore, when the co-workers go to help the saints, it is important to have a strong spirit, be "thick-skinned," and not have any opinions. We must learn to practice these three things. We want every brother and sister to eventually be a prophet and a teacher. We must go against the way of Christianity, which is to annul the gifts and function of the saints by focusing on one pastor who does everything. This is not according to the Bible. However, we must admit that even though there is much light among us, our practice is not strong. I believe it is the Lord's good pleasure that every brother and sister have a turn and function. We hope that after meeting in this way for half a year to one year, every brother and sister will be able to speak, that is, to function as a prophet and a teacher. Everything depends on our endeavoring.

If during 1985 there is a onefold increase in Taipei or,

better yet, a twofold increase, there will be more than one thousand small groups, and this will require the help of more than a thousand full-timers. Therefore, it is likely that in the future we will need all the part-time serving ones to help. In addition, some of the brothers and sisters currently meeting in the small groups can help. In a strong local church every brother and sister is useful and capable of going out to battle and of functioning as a prophet and a teacher. When he opens his mouth, his spirit is released, and he is thick-skinned, that is, not self-conscious. Moreover, he does not have any opinions, and will not cause disputes or engage in arguments with others.

ALWAYS HAVING LIGHT FROM THE TRUTH
AND THE SUPPLY OF LIFE
IN THE FELLOWSHIP OF THE SMALL GROUPS

I believe that this demonstration has given us an impression. When we participate in the small group gatherings, we should not forget the impression that we have received. This should be a model. We should forsake idle talk, concentrate on reading the Bible, and be familiar with the footnotes. However, in the meetings we should not read the footnotes in a rigid way; it is sufficient to read only the main points. Nor is it necessary to read every paragraph in a Life-study message. If we prepare before the meeting, we can select portions. This will save time in the meeting and help everyone focus. If too many points are touched in one meeting, everyone's attention will dissipate. In every meeting we must learn to bring the saints into the light in the truth and the life supply so that the brothers and sisters are fed when they leave.

This kind of fellowship in the small groups must take place at least every other week, and the other meetings in the small groups can be used to preach the gospel. It would be quite substantial if in twenty-six gatherings a year the light from the truth is released and life is supplied. In the meetings we must be filled in spirit. Those of us who have more growth in life must bear the responsibility to pray and be filled with a praying spirit. As soon as the meeting begins, our spirit should come forth. Basketball is a good example.

You cannot be courteous when the ball comes. Rather, you should forget your self-consciousness, your face, and everything else, and concentrate on the ball and getting it into the hoop. The focus is on scoring points. It is the same in a small group meeting. As soon as we arrive at the meeting, we should forget about everything else and only remember our spirit. Our spirit is the ball. We should also remember to release the light in the truth and to supply the riches of life. Our goal is for every attendant, including ourselves, to be enlightened and supplied.

CHAPTER FIVE

THE SUPPLY OF TRUTH AND LIFE
IN THE SMALL GROUP MEETINGS AND
THE PRACTICE OF
THE BREAD-BREAKING MEETING

THE SUPPLY OF TRUTH AND LIFE
IN THE SMALL GROUP MEETINGS

Not Being Too Rigid in Using the Footnotes
in the Recovery Version

I would like to call your attention to one matter. You may
use the Life-study messages and the Recovery Version in the
small groups, but when you use the footnotes, you should not
be too rigid. This is because some footnotes are there to
explain the meaning of certain words. For instance, in explain-
ing the word *holy* in Romans 1:2, footnote 3 mentions several
terms, such as *holiness, saints,* and *sanctified.* In a small
group meeting, you should not bring out all these terms. As
long as you understand that *holy* means to be separated unto
God, it is enough. Some footnotes were written in detail
because we need to base the explanation of a word on a
proper source and cannot explain it without any foundation.
When you use the Life-study messages in the small groups,
the less you explain the meaning of the words the better. If
some saints desire to know more, they can study by themselves.

Spending Time to Find Out the Major Points
in a Life-study Message

Life-study messages may contain some words of expla-
nation, which you do not need to read through in their entirety.
Therefore, before a meeting we must spend time in the
Life-study message that will be covered. As we are preparing

the message, we can mark the parts that we feel should be used in the meeting. We must find the major points, and then during the meeting the saints can read a few sections related to the central point. There may be the need to explain some points to help enliven the meeting. If the message is read rigidly, the atmosphere of the meeting will be stiff, and it will be difficult for the saints to have a taste for the message and to enter into the enjoyment.

Having Spontaneous Fellowship

After the major points are read and the central point is emphasized with a brief explanation, there can be some spontaneous fellowship. We all must exercise in this matter. We should not be overconfident and think that this is not important. In this new beginning with the small groups in the church, we all need to exercise. Whether we are a full-timer, a part-timer, an elder, or a deacon, we must exercise in the small groups.

Exercising to Diligently Prepare Material

Before every small group meeting, we must be diligent to read the text and the footnotes in the Recovery Version and also the related portion in the Life-study messages. If we practice marking the places that should be used in the meeting, after six months to a year, we will be experienced and proficient. We should not go to the small group to give an inspirational message; rather, we should learn to apply the material that we have.

Some may think that this practice is regulated and not according to the Spirit. However, it is not simple to do things according to the Spirit. In the fellowship meeting of a small group, we must always have the Lord's word; otherwise, there is no focus. We are not experienced enough to speak without preparation; therefore, we need to prepare the material. We cannot find material that is as complete as the Recovery Version and the Life-study messages. However, we do not need to be a tape recorder and mechanically recite what is in the books. Rather, we should be chefs that use the material in the books to prepare a delicious dish. We even do not need to buy groceries, because all the material is found in the footnotes of the Recovery Version and in the Life-studies. We only need to study to determine what portions in the Life-study should be used in the meeting.

The footnotes of the Recovery Version and the Life-study messages are in our hands. There is no stipulation that we can use only one message; we simply need to pray concerning which paragraphs to use. From a message of fifteen pages, we might select only three pages to read in the meeting. As we fellowship with the saints, we can explain certain portions. In this way the message becomes living, full of light, and full of the life supply. If every small group would pursue and enter into the truth in this way, it will be easier for the elders to lead the church, and the church will advance.

Releasing the Light from the Truth and Supplying the Riches of Life in Every Meeting

Suppose we use the Life-study of Romans. The content is rich and inexhaustible, but when we release the light from the truth and supply the riches of life in the small group, we do not have to present every point. As long as there is some light and some of the riches of life are supplied, our goal is achieved. We do not need to learn the entire book of Romans as if we were a theologian. The food that we need is in the *Life-study of Romans.* We can select portions from the Life-study for the saints to read. Even if the saints do not understand the Epistle to the Romans, as they continue to attend the meetings, they will be enlightened and supplied with life from the riches in the book of Romans. In this way, the goal of the small group meeting will be attained. This brief instruction requires our practice.

THE PRACTICE OF
THE BREAD-BREAKING MEETING

We will now consider how to have the bread-breaking meeting. We may think that we are experienced, but the structure of our meetings is not definite and clear. Every meeting should have a structure, and the bread-breaking meeting is no exception. The focus of the bread-breaking meeting is the remembrance of the Lord, but it is not to remember the Lord's death—it is to remember the Lord Himself (1 Cor. 11:24-25). When we remember the Lord, we are declaring His death (v. 26); that is, we display, exhibit, the Lord's death. However, we do not remember the Lord's death; instead, we remember the Lord Himself.

Remembering the Lord Being to Enjoy the Lord

Remembering the Lord is to enjoy the Lord. In the night that the Lord Jesus was betrayed, He "took bread, and having given thanks, He broke it and said, This is My body, which is given for you; this do unto the remembrance of Me" (vv. 23b-24). These verses show that to remember the Lord is to eat the Lord. Verse 25 says, "Similarly also the cup after they had dined, saying, This cup is the new covenant established in My blood; this do, as often as you drink it, unto the remembrance of Me." The focus of remembering the Lord is the enjoyment of the Lord, who became flesh, passed through death and resurrection, and ascended. In the bread-breaking meeting there are two symbols on the table: the bread, signifying the Lord's body, and the cup, signifying the Lord's blood. The fact that the body and the blood are separated signifies the Lord's death. Hence, in the bread-breaking meeting, we remember the incarnated Lord, who passed through human living on the earth and entered into death. Then He resurrected, ascended to the heights, and became the life-giving Spirit to produce us, the many sons of God, as His Body. We remember the Lord by enjoying Him as such a Lord. This should be the center of our hymns and prayers.

I attended a bread-breaking meeting in which a sister called the hymn "Revive Thy Work, O Lord" (*Hymns,* #797). This hymn is not appropriate for the bread-breaking meeting. Perhaps the sister had a feeling for the hymn because the church was promoting the burden of preaching the gospel and gaining people. However, when we come to the bread-breaking meeting to remember the Lord, we should remember the Lord and enjoy Him. As we enjoy Him, He is enjoying us; if we do not enjoy Him, He cannot enjoy us. The more we enjoy Him the more He enjoys us. Hence, we must remember that in the bread-breaking meeting we should not think of anything other than the Lord. This is something we all must learn.

The more experienced saints should spontaneously express a proper pattern in the bread-breaking meeting; otherwise, less experienced saints will not maintain the focus of the meeting. The more experienced saints should bear the responsibility for the direction of the meeting.

The Experienced Saints Needing to Direct the Meeting

In every meeting there is always the operating of the Spirit; nevertheless, the Holy Spirit still needs an outlet. Sometimes the outlet is through prayers and praises, and other times it is through the hymns. Last year in a training in Irving, Texas, we had a bread-breaking meeting. In that meeting I sensed that the Spirit was operating, and I waited, but no one made a move. Therefore, I called *Hymns,* #132: "Lo! in heaven Jesus sitting, / Christ the Lord is there enthroned; / As the man by God exalted, / With God's glory He is crowned." As soon as this hymn was sung, the entire meeting was released, and we were in the heavens.

In every bread-breaking meeting there is a need for the more experienced saints to follow the operation of the Holy Spirit and to lead the meeting according to this operation. The church is like a family with many generations meeting together. The older saints should not constantly reminiscence about the old days, saying that it was like such and such "in the early days." Neither should the younger ones be at a loss concerning the structure of the meetings. The more experienced saints should learn how to "steer" the meeting. This is different from controlling. It is to be at the "helm" of a meeting and to steer it in an appropriate direction. This is not control.

If the experienced saints in the church can be at the "helm" of the bread-breaking meeting, the meeting will progress steadily according to a proper pattern. Then the saints, including those who have been recently recovered back to the church life as well as those who have been newly saved, will be under the nurturing and cultivating of the pattern in the meetings, and they will be raised up in their experience.

The First Section
Being to Remember the Lord and
the Second Section
Being to Worship the Father

The pattern of remembering the Lord in a local church is our family inheritance. The first section of the bread-breaking meeting is to remember the Lord, and the second section is to worship the Father. According to Matthew 26:30, after the Lord Jesus established His supper, He led the disciples to sing a hymn. This means that after leading the disciples to remember Him, the Lord led them to worship the Father. Hebrews 2:12 says, "I will declare Your name to My brothers; in the midst of the church I will sing hymns of praise to You." This clearly points out that in the Lord's resurrection, He is leading His many brothers to worship the Father. We should not be indifferent concerning the second section, in which we worship the Father. We should spend ten to fifteen minutes to properly worship the Father with prayer, praises, and hymns. During the second section of the meeting, we should take the Father as the center.

After there has been much worship and praise to the Father, it is inappropriate to call a hymn concerning the Lord's precious blood. Hymns concerning the Lord's precious blood should be sung while the Lord is remembered and not during the worship of the Father. It may be that a newly recovered saint, who has an appreciation for the Lord's precious blood and does not know the difference between praising the Lord and worshipping the Father, calls the hymn. In this case we should sing the hymn and not change it; otherwise, he may not come to another meeting. As he continues to attend the meetings, he will understand the difference between praising the Lord and worshipping the Father.

Testimonies Needing
to Follow the Flow of the Spirit

When we give a testimony in the bread-breaking meeting,

we must learn to sense the atmosphere of the meeting and not interrupt it. The meeting may progress to a stage where it requires prayer. If our spirit is keen, when someone begins to pray, we will realize the need for more prayer. We should not call another hymn, because this will dissipate the atmosphere of prayer, and it will be difficult to continue the prayer after singing a hymn. Therefore, we must develop a spirit of prayer.

To give a testimony during the bread-breaking meeting, one must follow the flow of the Spirit. This does not mean that you should not give a testimony before the bread or the cup is passed, but that you must have the assurance that your testimony will not interrupt the meeting. If you do not have the assurance, it is better to wait until after the remembrance of the Lord and the worship of the Father before you give a testimony. The bread-breaking meeting usually lasts about one and a half to two hours after which there is still twenty to thirty minutes for the brothers and sisters to fellowship.

PREPARING FOR INCREASE

If we expect the number of saints in the church to increase twofold, the number of small groups should also increase twofold. At present there are three hundred sixty groups; a twofold increase means an increase of another three hundred sixty groups. Every month we should add thirty groups. The responsible brothers in the twenty-one halls should begin to prepare and plan how to divide the halls into districts and groups. As the number of saints increases, there is the need to add more groups. There is also the need to decide which groups should come together in districts to break bread. Besides this, there should also be a way to keep attendance so that we know who comes to the meetings regularly. We should also consider where the groups should meet.

I hope that all the halls will consider and observe this matter so that you may know which groups should be combined together to have a bread-breaking meeting, how many bread-breaking meetings there should be, and where the meetings can be held. In addition to the bread-breaking meeting, we also need prayer meetings. There are twenty-one halls in the church in Taipei, but there are only seven hundred saints in the prayer meetings. Hence, we should also consider which groups should be combined. The responsible ones in the halls and the experienced saints in the groups must consider how to carry out the bread-breaking meeting as well as the prayer meeting in the groups. Not every small group will have a prayer meeting.

KNOWING THE ESSENTIAL AND ECONOMICAL ASPECTS OF THE TRIUNE GOD

We have considered the two sections of the bread-breaking meeting: for the remembrance of the Lord and the worship of the Father. We will now consider the person of the Trinity. There is an essential and an economical aspect of the Triune God. Due to the fact that some theologians did not have a clear view concerning these two aspects, the essential aspect and the economical aspect of the Triune God, great mistakes have been made in church history.

The Father, the Son, and the Spirit Being Distinct but Inseparable

Based on the revelation of the Bible, Bible teachers throughout the centuries have used the noun *Trinity* and the adjective *Triune*. Since human language is based on human culture, if there is no culture, words will not be produced to match it. For example, two hundred years ago there was no telephone; thus, the word *telephone* did not exist. With the invention of the telephone, a word was produced. In recent years the culture of computers has pervaded society, and as a result, many terms associated with computers were created to express and transmit this culture. In the same way, much progress has been made in studying the truths in the Bible; therefore, there is a need to create new terms to express these truths.

On the one hand, the Bible shows that God is one; on the other hand, the Bible shows the Father, the Son, and the Spirit. Are the Father, the Son, and the Spirit three persons? This is truly not easy to explain, because the Father, the Son, and the Spirit are distinct but inseparable. If we separate Them, we have three Gods. This is the teaching of tritheism.

The Father, the Son, and the Spirit cannot be separated. Isaiah 9:6 says, "A child is born to us, / A Son is given to us; / ...His name will be called / Wonderful Counselor, / Mighty God, / Eternal Father." The child who was born to us is the Mighty God, and the Son who was given to us is the Eternal Father. First Corinthians 15:45 says that Christ the Son, who passed through death and resurrection, is the last Adam who became the life-giving Spirit. Second Corinthians 3:17 also says that the Lord is the Spirit. By putting these verses together, we see that the Father, the Son, and the Spirit are one.

God Being One but Having the Aspect of Being Three

Some people overstress the aspect of God being three and deny the aspect of the Father, the Son, and the Spirit being one. Hence, they fall into the error of tritheism. Orthodox theologians have seen that God is one and yet has the aspect of being three. Hence, they invented the term *Trinity*. The Trinity is a mystery which no one can clearly explain. Bible scholars and theologians over the centuries all agree that God is one, but there is indeed the aspect of His being three. Although they have spent a great deal of time to study the Trinity, they cannot clearly differentiate between His being one and His being three, but they all admit that God is one yet three.

The three of the Triune God are distinct but inseparable. On the one hand, the Father, the Son, and the Spirit are distinct, but on the other hand, the Son is the Father, and the Son is also the Spirit; the three are inseparable. The Lord Jesus said, "I am in the Father and the Father is in Me" (John 14:10). He also said, "I and the Father are one" (10:30). Although the Son and the Father are one, there is still a distinction of "I" and "the Father." There is a distinction between the Father and the Son, but we cannot separate the two, because the two are one and cannot be separated. How are the Father and the Son distinct? And to what extent are They distinct? It is difficult to explain clearly. Orthodox theologians only say that God is three and yet one, and that there is a distinction between the three. If we say that there is no distinction between the three, we will fall into the error of modalism.

God Being One Essentially in His Existence and Being Three Economically for His Move

With regard to the essential aspect of the Triune God, He is revealed as one, and with regard to the economical aspect, He is revealed as three. Economically, the Father and the Son are distinct, but essentially, the Father and the Son are one. The essential aspect refers to His existence, whereas the economical aspect refers to His move. Based on the verses that we quoted from the Scriptures, the Father, the Son, and the Spirit are one. The Son is the Father, and the Son is the Spirit. In essence the Father, the Son, and the Spirit are one.

Tritheists stress the aspect of God being three but neglect the aspect of God being one. They quote verses such as Matthew 3:16-17 and John 17:1 to prove that the Father and the Son are distinct and separate. However, these verses refer to the economical aspect of the Triune God. The Father, the Son, and the Spirit are economically distinct but essentially one.

On the Lord's Day we break bread to remember the Lord, and we follow the Son to worship the Father. This is economical. Are the Father, the Son, or the Spirit in us? The answer is that all three are in us, but the three are one. This is essential. As we worship the Father, we are following the Son, the firstborn Son of God, who is leading many sons to worship the Father; this is economical. When we worship, there is a distinction between the Son and the Father. This is not a matter of essence; it is related to God in His economy. After we remember the Lord, we follow Him to worship the Father. This is not with regard to the essential Trinity but with regard to His move in His economy. In God's move there is a distinction between the Father and the Son. The Son was crucified on the cross, because crucifixion is a move in God's economy. However, according to His existence, the Son is not merely the Son; the Son is also the Father and the Spirit (Col. 1:19; 2:9). Economically, the One who was crucified was the Son; essentially, however, the Triune God was crucified.

CHAPTER SIX

THE WORSHIP OF THE FATHER
IN THE LORD'S TABLE MEETING
AND SOME MATTERS
RELATED TO THE PRAYER MEETING

REMEMBERING THE LORD
AND WORSHIPPING THE FATHER
IN THE LORD'S TABLE MEETING

For our fellowship concerning the worship of the Father, which is in the second section of the Lord's table meeting, let us read Matthew 26:29-30: "I say to you, I shall by no means drink of this product of the vine from now on until that day when I drink it new with you in the kingdom of My Father. And after singing a hymn, they went out to the Mount of Olives." Verse 29 reveals what the Lord Jesus said after He established His supper. Verse 30 begins, "After singing a hymn..." This simple statement implies a great deal. There are three questions that we need to consider with this statement. First, who sang the hymn? Second, to whom did they sing in praise? And third, why did they sing? According to the context, the Lord Jesus and His disciples sang a hymn, and they sang it in praise to the Father. Immediately after the Lord established His supper, He and His disciples sang hymns of praise to the Father. The significance of this is deep.

When the Lord established His supper in verses 26 to 28, His desire was that His disciples remember Him. This is according to 1 Corinthians 11:24, which says, "This do unto the remembrance of Me." The Lord told His disciples that the central point of the table meeting is the remembrance of Him. However, whenever the Son did something in the New Testament, He never forgot the Father. If in establishing His supper, the Lord had only said, "Do this in remembrance of Me," He would not have expressed anything of the Father to the disciples. Therefore, the phrase *after singing a hymn* implies something of deep significance. It indicates that after the disciples remembered the Lord, He led them to sing and praise the Father. This is the worship to the Father.

Although the phrase *after singing a hymn* is simple, many times simple phrases in the Bible express important points. When the Lord Jesus established His supper, He was burdened, preparing to deliver Himself into the hands of those who would kill Him. Therefore, He took the opportunity before He was killed to establish His supper for His disciples to remember Him. If He had stopped there and had then gone to the Garden of Gethsemane and delivered Himself to those who would kill Him, the disciples would not have been led to the Father. Hence, the Lord's leading the disciples to sing praise to God was to leave them with the impression that they must not forget to worship the Father when they remember Him.

The Lord Singing Hymns of Praise to the Father with His Brothers in the Midst of the Church

Hebrews 2:11-12 says, "Both He who sanctifies and those who are being sanctified are all of One, for which cause He is not ashamed to call them brothers, saying, 'I will declare Your name to My brothers; in the midst of the church I will sing hymns of praise to You.'" The thought in these verses follows Matthew 26:29-30. After the Lord established His supper, He sang a hymn with His disciples to praise the Father. This was to impress them with the matter that even after remembering Him, they should worship the Father. Then the Lord died on the cross and resurrected after three days. In His resurrection many brothers were produced. Before the Lord's resurrection He had only disciples, not brothers. First Peter 1:3 says that we were regenerated through His resurrection. Hence, when the Lord Jesus saw Mary on the morning of His resurrection, He said, "Do not touch Me, for I have not yet ascended to the Father; but go to My brothers and say to them, I ascend to My Father and your Father, and My God and your God" (John 20:17). As the only begotten Son of God, the Lord Jesus was born to be the firstborn Son of God on the day of His resurrection. In His resurrection all those who believe into Him were also begotten as the many sons of God, His many brothers.

Hebrews 2:11 says that the Lord Jesus, the One who sanctifies, is one with His brothers, the sanctified ones, because both He and we are born of the Father. Verse 11 also says, "For which cause He is not ashamed to call them brothers." This verse can be compared to John 20:17, where the Lord said, "Go to My brothers." At that time the disciples were weak. On the night that the Lord Jesus was betrayed, Peter denied the Lord three times (Matt. 26:69-75; Mark 14:66-72; Luke 22:55-62; John 18:15-18, 25-27), and the others were disappointed and fled. This was to their shame. They were not worthy to be called brothers, but the Lord was not ashamed of them. Because of what the Lord accomplished on the morning of His resurrection, He was not ashamed to call them His brothers.

The last portion of Hebrews 2:12 says, "In the midst of the church I will sing hymns of praise to You." Here *You* refers to the Father. Hence this portion can also be rendered, "In the midst of the church I will sing hymns of praise to the Father." In which Christian meeting is it most suitable for the Lord Jesus to sing hymns of praise to the Father in the midst of the church? By inference, this meeting must be the Lord's table meeting. Furthermore, after the Lord Jesus established His supper, when He led the disciples to sing a hymn, He was not inside of them, because He had not yet resurrected and could not enter into them. However, on the morning of the Lord's resurrection, all the disciples became the Lord's brothers. On the evening of the same day the Lord entered into the disciples by breathing into them (John 20:22). From that time onward whenever the disciples met together, the Lord was with them. Hence, the Lord singing hymns of praise in the midst of the church means that He sings within His brothers. And without a doubt, such singing of praise is most appropriate in the Lord's table meeting.

THE TRUE WORSHIP TO THE TRIUNE GOD
IN THE NEW TESTAMENT

This light was not seen until the nineteenth century when the Brethren were raised up in England. They emphasized the truth according to 2 Timothy 2:15, which speaks of cutting straight the word of the truth. In their study of the Word, they found out that the New Testament worship consists of the remembrance of the Lord and the worship of the Father. This is not like presenting offerings by killing bulls and sheep in the Old Testament. Rather, it is the believers coming to the Lord's table and taking the Lord as everything to enjoy the Lord and thus remember Him. The true remembrance of the Lord is the enjoyment of the Lord. The more we enjoy Him, the more He is remembered. After we remember Him, we then praise the Father. This is the worship in the New Testament.

In the hymnal compiled by the Brethren, the first category in the table of contents is "Words of Praise." The contents of the first hymnal prepared by Brother Nee consisted entirely of hymns translated from the Brethren's hymnal, and the first category was also "Words of Praise." Some of the hymns were for the praise of the Father and others to praise the Lord. When we compiled the hymnal that we are using today, we put these hymns into two categories: one is the worship of the Father, and the other is the praise of the Lord. The light concerning the worship of the Father was first seen by the Brethren over one hundred fifty years ago and was passed on to us. Therefore, in the churches we break the bread to remember the Lord, and then we worship the Father. This is the true worship of the Triune God in the New Testament.

THE ESSENTIAL AND ECONOMICAL TRINITY

It seems that there is not much speaking in the New Testament concerning the worship of the Father. For this reason, we would like to give a further word of fellowship.

The Debate concerning the Trinity
and the Person of Christ

The Bible reveals that God is one and yet three. This is a

great revelation. God is unique, and His name is Jehovah. God is also three—the Father, the Son, and the Spirit. Ever since the second century, this issue has been a focal point of debate. The church fathers and early Bible scholars focused their study of the Bible on the Triune God and the person of Christ. They had different explanations and different views. The views of orthodox Bible scholars were more or less the same, but they could not come to a precise conclusion.

These debates continued for two centuries. In A.D. 325, when the Roman Empire ruled a vast territory and the Lord's gospel had spread over the entire Mediterranean region, the Emperor, Constantine the Great, felt that he had to resolve these doctrinal matters among Christians so that people of different ethnic backgrounds within the Empire could get along in complete harmony. Therefore, he ordered the main bishops to gather in Nicaea for a council in which he served as the chairman and exerted his political influence on all the parties. The conclusions of the council became the Nicene Creed. This creed is still taken as the fundamental belief in Catholicism and Protestantism.

The Nicene Creed speaks mainly of the person of Christ and the Triune God. We cannot say that the wording of the creed is not appropriate; however, its view is not as thorough, detailed, or complete as the Bible, because the Bible does not reveal the person of Christ and the Triune God by a set of articles but rather in a way that dispenses God into us as enjoyment. Therefore, the tone of the Bible is very sweet. For example, Isaiah 9:6 says, "A child is born to us, / A Son is given to us; /...And His name will be called /... Mighty God, / Eternal Father, / Prince of Peace." When these points, however, are written as articles in the creed, the complete, thorough, and sweet taste is altogether lost. As a result, man's understanding also fell short.

OUR STUDY

When the Brethren were raised up in the nineteenth century, they declared that they did not want any creed but the Bible, because the creeds had replaced the Bible. After the Brethren, other Christian groups made similar declarations.

Sixty years ago we also declared that we care only for the Bible, not the creeds. Since that time we have made an effort to study the person of Christ and the Triune God. In the initial period, I was very close to Brother Watchman Nee; you can say that we fought shoulder to shoulder in these matters. Hence, I know his beliefs, that is, what he believed concerning the person of Christ and the Triune God, and I agree fully with him. I inherited his view and have continued to study these issues until today. As a result, my study has become more thorough and detailed.

In 1949 I began the publishing work in Taipei; during that early period *The Ministry of the Word* magazine was the main publication. In 1960 I went to America and began to publish books in English in 1963. There are now a large number of publications, including the Life-study of the twenty-seven books of the New Testament. According to my estimation, during the past twenty-two years in America, I published more than three thousand messages, among which are the twelve hundred Life-study messages, comprising about one hundred twenty thousand pages, as well as about twenty thousand more pages in other books. The main topic of these books concerns the person of Christ and the Triune God. Around 1983 I came to the conclusion that the revelation in the Bible concerning the Triune God has two aspects, the essential aspect and the economical aspect. In other words, there is an essential aspect of the Trinity and an economical aspect of the Trinity.

The Essential Aspect Being with Regard to God's Existence, and the Economical Aspect Being with Regard to God's Move

The essential aspect speaks of God's existence, and the economical aspect speaks of God's move and God's work. The essential aspect of the Trinity relates to His existence, whereas the economical aspect of the Trinity relates to His move. Almost all the fundamental Bible scholars over the centuries acknowledge these two aspects: the essential and the economical. The essential aspect refers to the fact that the

Father, the Son, and the Spirit are one in existence. This is based on Isaiah 9:6, "A Son... / ...will be called /... Eternal Father," and also on 2 Corinthians 3:17, "The Lord is the Spirit." The Son is called the Father, and the Lord is the Spirit. Therefore, the Father, the Son, and the Spirit are one. This refers to His essence, His existence, not to His economy, His move.

Furthermore, it is also clearly stated in the New Testament that the Triune God has a move; that is, the Father made a plan, then the Son accomplished the Father's plan, and the Spirit applies the Son's accomplishment. These are the three steps of the move of the Triune God: the Father's plan, the Son's accomplishment, and the Spirit's application. For this reason, when the Son came out of the water, after He was baptized in the river Jordan, the Spirit descended upon Him like a dove and the Father spoke to Him from the heavens (Matt. 3:16-17). This is economical, not essential. In John 17:1, after the Lord spoke to the disciples, He lifted up His eyes to heaven and said, "Father, the hour has come; glorify Your Son that the Son may glorify You." This is the Son on earth praying to the Father in heaven; this does not refer to the essential aspect of the Trinity but to the economical aspect.

In the Lord's table meeting we first remember the Lord, and then we worship the Father. This is a matter of His economy. The essential aspect of the Triune God is for our experience and enjoyment; the economical aspect is for our service and worship. The Triune God dwelling in us emphasizes the aspect of His essence; our worshipping and serving the Triune God emphasize the aspect of His economy. We should never think that since the Father, the Son, and the Spirit are one, our worship of the Father is the same as our remembering the Lord. This can be compared to our calling "O Lord" or "O Father." In the table meeting we should never pray, "Father, thank You for shedding Your blood for me." Neither should we pray, "Father, You loved me so much that You even died for me." These prayers confuse the essential aspects of the Trinity with the economical aspects of the Trinity. This brief speaking is the essence of the studies in theology for the past two thousand years. It is altogether according to the Bible.

No matter how much Christianity is in confusion, our teaching is according to the sixty-six books of the pure Word of God. I have studied thoroughly almost every verse concerning the Triune God in these sixty-six books, and I have written many messages concerning the Triune God. Therefore, I am able to say in a simple and clear way that with respect to His existence, the Triune God has an essential aspect, and with respect to His move and work, the Triune God has an economical aspect. We need to enjoy Him and experience Him according to His essential aspect. We also need to serve Him and worship Him according to His economical aspect. Hence, in the table meeting we must follow the Spirit to remember the Lord, and then we must follow the Lord and the Spirit to worship the Father.

The last group of hymns in our hymnal under the category of "Worship of the Father" is titled "His Praise from Many Sons." This group of hymns is the highest. Many Christians do not understand what "His praise from many sons" means. It refers to the praise offered by the Lord Jesus together with His brothers. *Hymns,* #50 is in this group and contains deep truth concerning God's economy. It is a hymn of praise to the Father from many sons. This is related to God's economical aspect.

PRAYING WITH FASTING TO INCREASE
THE ATTENDANCE IN THE PRAYER MEETING

Because it is difficult to have a Christian prayer meeting, the attendance in the prayer meeting of almost all Christian groups is low. For this reason, it is our responsibility to find out how to increase the attendance in the prayer meeting. If each of us is revived in our spirit, the attendance in the prayer meeting will increase twofold. Every person who prays knows that individual prayer has a certain taste but that prayer in a meeting has a strong and rich taste. Therefore, I treasure my personal prayer, and I also treasure the prayer meeting; neither can replace the other. A person who prays much by himself will attend the prayer meeting. Hence, we cannot expect attendance in the prayer meeting to increase without spending time before the Lord by ourselves. We must ask the Lord for a revival: "O Lord, revive our gathering." We should even set aside time to fast and pray. In this way the number in the prayer meeting will increase.

EVERYONE WHO ATTENDS THE PRAYER MEETING NEEDING A SPIRIT OF PRAYER

For sixty years, from the time I was saved up to the present, I have been attending prayer meetings. First I attended prayer meetings in a denomination, then in a Brethren Assembly, and later in the prayer meetings of the church. According to my experience, everyone who comes to the prayer meeting must have a spirit of prayer. As soon as we step into the meeting, we should not care for anything but to pray. If someone is praying, we should wait until he finishes and then continue the prayer. We should not rely too much on the responsible brothers to lead the meeting. We should not expect them to call a hymn, open the prayer, or announce the items for prayer. Such a prayer meeting will not be strong.

In the prayer meetings of the churches in America, whoever arrives first begins to pray, and those who come later join in the prayer; everyone prays. No one waits until seven-thirty to begin praying, they do not sing first and then have an opening prayer, and there is neither a message nor an announcement concerning items for prayers. They just pray. This kind of prayer meeting is powerful and very living; oftentimes the prayer lasts for one and a half hours.

Generally speaking, if someone stands up to announce some items for prayer or to call a hymn in the middle of the prayer meeting, it is an interruption. The spirit of prayer should not be interrupted. Once it is interrupted, it is not easy to raise the meeting. Hence, when we come together to pray, we must take this as the goal. We should not rely on a program, nor should we depend on a few designated people. As soon as we come together, we should begin to pray.

Not Regarding the Prayer Meeting as a Routine

Someone may ask what we should pray for if the items for

prayer are not announced. Since we are all in the church life, we should know the needs of the church. When we come to the prayer meeting, we should not pray for trivial matters but for important matters, such as God's will, God's kingdom, and the propagation of the church. For instance, the church in Taipei is now at a turning point, a new beginning; we should pray earnestly for this. This does not mean, however, that no one should make a prayer request. If a family member is very sick, a saint can look for an opportunity to fellowship this matter by following the leading of the Holy Spirit. Then he can make a request for prayer.

The prayer meeting will be dead if we pray according to a list that is distributed to every hall or district. I am not saying that we should not have such a list but that it should not become a routine. When the brothers and sisters come together to pray, they should pray mainly for God's kingdom, the propagation of the gospel, and the building up of the church. Furthermore, they should also pray for the saints' growth in life and for the move of the church. These matters are our major concerns, and we should remember them in our prayer. If the elders, co-workers, and deacons realize that there is a crucial matter in the church that needs to be made known in the prayer meetings of the church, then it is proper to make an announcement. In addition, it is also good to allow the saints to fellowship some personal burdens. They may have a relative or a friend who needs to be saved and needs the intercession of the saints in the prayer meeting. This is acceptable. In any case, the prayer meeting should be living and not regarded as a routine.

Prayers Needing to Be Short yet Strong

Furthermore, there should not be long prayers. When I was young, I attended the prayer meeting of a Brethren assembly. Every time there were dozens of saints who would come to pray. Whenever one prayed, their prayer was very long; hence, many people dozed off on their knees. We should avoid this. Strong prayer is not usually long. I pray two sentences, another prays two sentences, and yet another follows by praying two sentences. After praying in this way for one item, we can move on to another item. In the end all the saints will pray as one man. This is the best prayer meeting. The more we pray, the more living the prayer becomes, and the more we pray, the higher and stronger the prayer becomes. We need to learn and exercise to have simple but strong and uplifting prayers. We should not worry about what to pray for next. The Holy Spirit will lead us to pray for different burdens one by one.

CHAPTER SEVEN

STUDYING THE TRUTHS
IN THE LORD'S RECOVERY

THE WORK OF THE FULL-TIMERS

The work of the full-time serving ones is mainly with the small groups in their respective localities. All full-timers must know how to help the small groups. We have already seen that the small group meeting is a fellowship meeting. A fellowship meeting is all-inclusive in nature. When a full-timer goes to a small group, he should not assume the status of a full-timer or display the air of a full-timer. In order to help the fellowship in a small group, he should first help the saints learn how to read the Word of God. The best materials for this are the Life-studies and the Recovery Version. Second, he should help them to gradually build up a proper bread-breaking meeting. Third, he should help them to attend the prayer meeting and learn to pray.

THE SPIRIT OF THE FULL-TIMERS

The full-timers do not hold a secular job. If possible, they should not be concerned about their food, their clothes, or their sleep. This is the spirit I had when I began to serve full time. I desired to use all my time to read the Bible, pray, fellowship with the Lord, pursue the Lord, serve the Lord, fellowship with the brothers and sisters, and preach the gospel. All the full-timers should have a spirit to consider the truth twenty-four hours a day. Often when I wake up in the morning, I immediately begin to consider the message that I gave the night before. I encourage the full-time serving ones to have such a mentality.

Although you brothers and sisters should not regard yourselves as full-timers or display the air of full-timers, the fact remains that this is your occupation. We have given up our education and jobs. We do not make money or seek prosperity in the world; we have given up all these things. Since this is our occupation, we should do an outstanding job. Of course, we should not be proud, but neither should we be without a backbone. Especially the young ones should never be careless about their food, clothing, or sleep.

In 1932 a denomination in Chefoo invited Brother Nee to give a message. I went along with him and stayed in a dormitory. The room I stayed in was so filthy that it was not suitable for sleeping; therefore, I spent a whole day cleaning the room. When others saw that the dormitory room was clean, they had a positive impression of the person who cleaned it. We should be such persons. If we are put in a place that is dirty, we should not merely accept it; rather, we should rise up to make the place clean and respectable. Hence, you must not be careless so that others do not despise your youth.

A BRIEF HISTORY OF THE RECOVERY OF THE TRUTH

Christianity Stressing Theology More Than the Bible

In a small group we will always encounter people who ask questions concerning the truth. Hence, we must have a thorough understanding of the truth so that we may be able to help them. In Christianity there is the Bible and there is theology. The Bible is God's revelation, but theology is the knowledge that men have gained from studying the Bible. The study of the Bible began in the second century after the apostles had died by the end of the first century. In the second century many lovers of the Lord and scholarly men were raised up by the Lord, and they began to study the Bible. The church fathers were produced from this group of people. For the past nineteen centuries the study of the Bible has never stopped. The results of these studies have been published and are the content of Christian theology.

The situation in Christianity today is pitiful because people pay more attention to theology than to the Bible. The truths that they accept are according to theology but are not necessarily according to the Bible. There are even several categories of theology. Catholicism has Catholic theology, and Protestant denominations have their own theological views. There is also the theology of modernists, who do not even believe that the Bible is God's revelation, that there are signs and wonders, or that the Lord Jesus is God possessing divinity.

The Brethren Thoroughly Studying the Bible

After the Brethren in England were raised up by the Lord in 1827, they began to study the Bible thoroughly instead of remaining in traditional theology. This was a great thing in church history. It was at that time that God used them to unfold many truths in the Bible. Within seventy-five years, in less than a century, they received much light from the Bible. During that period of time, a great amount of light came forth.

The Truths Taught by the Brethren
Influencing Christianity in America

The truths taught by the Brethren were accepted by Christianity in America, mainly through two persons. The first was D. L. Moody, who was a great evangelist in America in the nineteenth century. His teachings were all taken from the Brethren. Hence, the theology taught by Moody Bible Institute is based on the truths from the Brethren. The second person was Dr. C. I. Scofield. He was a well-known pastor in America who compiled and edited a reference Bible in which he adopted the teaching of the Brethren in almost ninety percent of the notes. Some of Scofield's contemporaries founded a seminary in Dallas, Texas, and its teaching of theology is based on Scofield's views. Hence, these two influential seminaries in America teach the Brethren theology.

From the second century until the nineteenth century, the study of theology was traditional. When the Brethren were raised up, however, they studied the Bible, consulting traditional theology, but they were not bound by tradition. As a result they received much light. It is regrettable that from the end of the nineteenth century until today, nearly a hundred years, the receiving of light has ceased, and the theology of the Brethren has become traditional. What does it mean to be traditional? To be traditional is to receive what has been passed down from our predecessors without seeing any new light from the Bible.

The Lord Continually Giving Us New Light for the Past Sixty Years

In China, however, the Lord raised up a person to receive new light. In 1920 Brother Watchman Nee was saved, and in 1922 a small gathering was raised up in his hometown. That was the first church in the Lord's recovery in China. For the past sixty years, our attitude has been to receive the help from our predecessors and to try our best to diligently research and study God's Word. In these sixty years the Lord has continually given us new light. For instance, the Western missionaries used the vague expression *three persons, one body* in reference to the Trinity, but no one explained what this meant. There is even a picture in the Eastern Orthodox Church portraying a person with one body and three heads. Later we discovered that this understanding was not according to the Bible, and we labored to study all the explanations and expositions concerning the Triune God in the Old and New Testaments.

In 1962 I arrived in America and began to release the results of the forty years of our studies. My intention was to lead the believers to experience the Triune God and to enjoy all the riches of Christ. I quoted Colossians 2:16-17: "Let no one therefore judge you in eating and in drinking or in respect of a feast or of a new moon or of the Sabbath, which are a shadow of the things to come, but the body is of Christ." Eating, drinking, feasting, and new moons are but shadows; the body is of Christ. I said that Christ is the reality of all the positive things in the universe; He is our real food, our real drink, our real clothing, our real feast, our real new moon, and our real rest. He is also our real air and real abode.

I was opposed and condemned as being pantheist because I said that Christ is all things. Since I also taught the saints to follow the inner sense of life in all matters, some condemned me and said that I was a mystic from the Far East. Their arbitrary view and criticism were based on their theology.

Our Study of the Word
Plus Our Experience of Life Issuing in the Truths Preached in the Lord's Recovery Today

What the missionaries from the West expounded influenced the truths that we initially released in the local churches. Gradually, we traced the truths back to the Bible. We read the Bible and studied the original Greek text. I used an interlinear Bible of Greek and English, purchased various reference books on the Greek text, and studied in depth the meaning of the Greek words in the Scriptures. In my home there are close to one hundred sets of books by different writers who are authorities on the Bible. For instance, there is a German writer named Gerhard Kittel whose work, *Theological Dictionary of the New Testament,* specializes in New Testament word studies. He expounded, word for word, the Greek words used in the New Testament. There are ten volumes in this set. One Greek word can have eight to ten pages of explanation, expounding in detail the classic usage of the Greek word, how it was used during the time of the Lord Jesus on the earth, its fundamental usage in the Bible, and its common usage by the Greeks. Nevertheless, we still examined this detailed information in light of the divine revelation. The footnotes in the Recovery Version were written according to this principle. We first studied the text of the Bible, and then based on our spiritual experience of the past decades, we produced footnotes and the Life-studies.

The truths that we heard and preached, from the beginning until today, are not bound by tradition. Instead, these truths have been identified according to the standard of the Bible. Not only so, we have studied the Bible thoroughly for decades. I dare not say that I have studied every word in the Old Testament, but I can say that I have studied every word in the New Testament. I wrote books that contain what I have gained from my studies according to a scholarly standard in which every finding is grounded with evidence. Although neither Brother Nee nor I studied in a seminary, no one can say that we do not know theology. We both advanced by standing on the shoulders of our predecessors. I share these things with you so that we may know the history of the truths among us.

THE ESSENTIAL AND THE ECONOMICAL TRINITY

The saints in the Lord's recovery should learn the truths concerning the essential and economical aspects of the Trinity. *Essential* refers to the constitution and the existence of God, which is God Himself. A person's constitution and existence are himself. The essential aspect of the Trinity speaks of the person of the Triune God. The term *economical* refers to an intention, a plan, or an arrangement. Undoubtedly, this refers to God's move, acts, and work. Whereas the essential aspect of the Trinity refers to God's constitution, God's existence, and God Himself, the economical aspect of the Trinity refers to God's plan, God's intention, God's arrangement, God's move, God's acts, and God's work.

Essence Referring to God Himself, whereas *Economy* Referring to God's Works

To put it simply, *essence* refers to God Himself, and *economy* refers to His work. God the Father had a plan in eternity past. According to this plan, He chose us and predestinated us (Eph. 1:3-6). Not only so, in eternity past God the Father ordained that His Son would become a man, die on behalf of men, and accomplish God's redemption (vv. 7-12). God also ordained that the Spirit would apply to us what God the Father planned and what God the Son accomplished (vv. 13-14). This is God's economy; it is God's plan, God's work, and God's move.

When the Son of God, the Lord Jesus, came to be a man on the earth, everything He did was economical. When He was baptized in the river Jordan, the Holy Spirit descended upon Him, and God the Father spoke from the heavens (Matt. 3:16-17); this was economical. With regard to His economy, there is the aspect of the move of the three of the Triune God—the Father, the Son, and the Spirit. Furthermore, the Triune God works in three stages. The Father planned before the foundation of the world. The Son accomplished what the Father planned in the four Gospels. The Spirit's application takes place in Acts and the Epistles. We can clearly see three consecutive steps. The first step is the Father's plan, the second step is the Son's accomplishment of the Father's plan, and the third step is the Spirit's application of the Son's accomplishment of the Father's plan. These three steps are not related to God's essence but to His economy.

The Twofoldness of the Truths in the Bible

When the Lord Jesus was on the earth, He often prayed to God the Father. In Matthew 11:25-26 He prayed, "I extol You, Father, Lord of heaven and of earth, because You have hidden these things from the wise and intelligent and have revealed them to infants. Yes, Father, for thus it has been well-pleasing in Your sight." Then in 27:46 when He was on the cross, He prayed, "My God, My God, why have You forsaken Me?" The Son prayed to the Father; this indicates that the Son and the Father are distinct. This is the economical aspect.

The truths in the Bible are of two sides; anything that exists in the universe has two sides. Even a thin sheet of paper has two sides: the front and the back. Our head also has two sides: the front has seven holes, and the back has none. We could never come to a conclusion as to what a person looks like if we see him only from the front or the back. Hence, on the one hand, the Lord Jesus stood in the water, and the Father spoke from heaven (3:16-17). On the other hand, Isaiah 9:6 says, "A Son is given to us; / ... And His name will be called / ... Eternal Father." The Son is called the Father, indicating that the Son is the Father. This shows the twofoldness of the truth.

When the Lord Jesus was on the earth, His disciple Philip said to Him, "Lord, show us the Father and it is sufficient for us" (John 14:8). Philip seemed to be saying, "We understand that You are the Son. We see You every day, but we are not satisfied. We want to see the Father. If You could show us the Father, we would be content." After hearing this, the Lord Jesus said, "Have I been so long a time with you, and you have not known Me, Philip? He who has seen Me has seen the Father; how is it that you say, Show us the Father?" (v. 9). The Lord seemed to be saying, "You have seen Me for more than three years. How can you say that you have not seen the Father? Why is it you still do not know that when you see Me, you see the Father? Why do you still ask Me to show you the Father? Why do you still not know that I am in the Father?" The Lord then said, "I am in the Father and the Father is in Me" (v. 10). Hence, we can say that when the Lord Jesus was praying on the earth to the Father in heaven, He was in the Father, and when the Father in heaven listened to Him praying on earth, the Father was in the Son. The Lord said, "I and the Father are one" (10:30). Isaiah 9:6 says that the Son is called the Father. Second Corinthians 3:17 says, "The Lord is the Spirit." Therefore, the Father, the Son, and the Spirit are one. This is the word in the Bible.

The Bible also speaks of "the last Adam" (1 Cor. 15:45b). The last Adam is the incarnated Lord, who passed through death and resurrection to become the life-giving Spirit. If we say that the life-giving Spirit is not the Holy Spirit, then is there a second Spirit who came to give life besides the Holy Spirit? This is heresy. The life-giving Spirit is definitely the Holy Spirit.

The Bible has two sides. On the one hand, it speaks of the economical aspect of the Trinity in relation to God's move, God's work. On the other hand, it speaks of the essential aspect of the Trinity in relation to God Himself, God's existence. When the Lord Jesus came to the earth to accomplish God's work, He stood in the water; this was part of His move. When the Spirit descended like a dove, this was also part of His move, and when the Father spoke from the heavens, this was part of His move. The Lord praying to the Father in heaven was also a move, a work. All these are related to God's economical aspect. In God's economy and in His essence, the Father, the Son, and the Spirit are distinct but not separate. The three are one.

CHAPTER EIGHT

THE PROPER AGGRESSIVENESS OF THE LORD'S SERVING ONES

BEING AGGRESSIVE IN LEARNING TO SERVE THE LORD

The purpose of this training is for the full-time serving ones to learn to receive a burden. In order for you to help the small groups, you must realize the need for learning. You should not expect to accomplish something in a quick way or even to do something well in your first attempt. God creates, but man must study. To study means to learn. Whoever expects to do something well in his first attempt will not achieve success. In the story of the tortoise and the hare, the capable hare lost the race, whereas the incapable tortoise won. If we desire to succeed in anything, we must be like the tortoise; we must be patient and willing to spend time to labor persistently.

After finishing the training, you must concentrate on reading the Bible and the Life-study messages from Monday to Friday for four hours every morning. Then, depending on the arrangement in your locality, you should serve in coordination with the church in the afternoon. You must also set aside some time to review your notes from the training. Furthermore, seven hours of sleep should be sufficient. If you usually sleep eight hours and do not have time to review your notes, you can sleep for seven and a half hours and use thirty minutes to review your notes or to consider how to help your small group. This can be compared to playing basketball. Even if you receive instructions from a coach, you will not know how to play properly if you do not practice. We need time for practice.

My greatest concern when a person begins to serve the Lord is that he may become useless. "I am serving the Lord, not men" becomes a slogan that he hides behind in order to not improve himself. The denominations in Christianity have a system of examinations and promotions, but we do not have any examinations or promotions. Therefore, it is easy for full-timers to neglect to improve themselves. In today's society, if a person is not aggressive, he will not be promoted, nor will he be able to keep his job. Since World War II the whole world has been advancing. If a person is not aggressive to learn, he will lose his job and also fall far behind as the world progresses. Hence, I encourage you to exercise your spirit and to exercise a strong will to be aggressive in your service to the Lord. You must be aggressive; otherwise, after serving full time for six months, you will be useless. Even if you do not take the way of serving full time, you need to be aggressive and seek to advance in your job; otherwise, you will be eliminated. If this is the situation in the world, we should be even more aggressive in serving the Lord.

A PERSONAL TESTIMONY

All the young serving ones should be aggressive. There is no limit to being aggressive. Every occupation has specialized knowledge, and no one is born with this knowledge. After I had been saved for seven years, the Lord raised up a church in my hometown in 1932. It was my responsibility to release messages in the meetings since I had learned some truths. The more I spoke, the more there was a need to speak, and the more there was a need, the more I spoke. Gradually I discovered that depending on the Chinese Union Bible and the King James Version of the Bible as my only reference books was not sufficient to meet the need, because many items of the truth required the defining of doctrine. The Chinese Union Version is a smooth and elegant translation, and its language is full of rhythm; however, in some places it lacks accuracy. In order to determine whether its translation is accurate, I could not rely on English Bibles; I needed to base my judgment of the words in the Bible on the original languages.

At that time I wrote to a brother in Shanghai and requested that he go to a Christian bookstore to purchase a copy of an English-Greek interlinear Bible for me, which I received at the end of 1932. Before then I had not learned the Greek alphabet, but a copy of the New Testament in Chinese that I received from an elderly brother included an explanation of the Greek language. The first page of this explanation consisted of the Greek alphabet with a pronunciation guide in both Mandarin and English. I used this to learn the Greek alphabet in six months.

Gradually I discovered that the English translation in the English-Greek interlinear Bible does not always convey the right meaning. In every language there are often words that have more than one meaning. For this reason, I needed a Greek dictionary to understand the Greek. When Japan invaded China, the Japanese army put many Western missionaries into concentration camps and sold their books. I took the opportunity and purchased many used books, including two excellent Greek-English dictionaries. I used these books to learn Greek.

During the fifty-two years that have passed since 1932, I have done in-depth study of biblical Greek using the writings of biblical scholars throughout the centuries, even though I have not studied Greek in any school. I regularly consult Greek dictionaries and Bible concordances. One of these works, *Theological Dictionary of the New Testament,* is a ten-volume set by a German brother, Gerhard Kittel. This dictionary lists and explains every Greek word according to its usage in the ancient times, in the New Testament times, and in modern times. I consult this set of books the most. As a result I can cut straight the word of the truth according to the Greek language when I expound the New Testament.

BEING AGGRESSIVE
IN LEARNING EVERYTHING
RELATED TO SERVING THE LORD

We must be aggressive. I hope that the young people who are serving full time will study Greek. There are even good videotapes available that teach Greek. In order to serve the

Lord, you must be immersed in the Lord's Word and spend time in it. Hence, you must learn some Greek. Some may wonder when they can find the time to learn Greek. You can find the time to learn Greek by spending less time for your meals, your sleep, talking on the phone, conversing, and reading the newspaper. Saving time in this way is what the Scriptures call "redeeming the time" (Eph. 5:16). For example, it is important to know the world situation, but for this there is a need to read only the international section of the newspaper.

Since I understand the Bible and the truth, and I also know history, I know the spiritual application of history. The book *The World Situation and God's Move* proves that I have a thorough understanding of world history. Hence, you need to study a little history and know the world situation. This will help you in serving the Lord. If you know history and the world situation, you will understand people and different circumstances. Young people should have this kind of training. You must be aggressive. The more you learn, the more useful you will be.

You should not rely on the diploma from your school; instead, you should study hard and be aggressive. You are still young and full of potential. Your time is precious; you must redeem every minute by learning everything related to serving the Lord. In addition to Chinese, you should study at least two other languages: Greek and English. This will help you.

You should also be aggressive to learn how to converse with others and how to speak for the Lord. You should learn how to have the proper attitude, expression, and gestures when you converse with others. I have studied all these matters. In 1927 I realized that I would spend my whole life preaching the Lord's word. I did not study theology, nor did I study methods of preaching, but I came up with two ways to practice—I would preach to the ocean, and I would stand before a mirror and practice preaching. This practice helped me greatly. When it was time for me to stand up to give a message, everyone was surprised and asked where I had learned to speak. I also learned how to contact others and to use proper mannerisms in greeting or shaking hands with others so that I could earn others' respect

You should not think that these matters are unrelated to serving the Lord. When we go out to contact people, our attitude, expression, speaking, and conduct have much to do with serving the Lord. If we are proper in these aspects, we will give others the impression that we are a weighty person who does not act rashly or frivolously. Thus, what we say will be taken into consideration by others. Our work consists of nothing but speaking with others to help and to enlighten them. If the way we speak or conduct ourselves is not acceptable, no matter what we say, others will have a negative impression of us, and this will nullify everything. Therefore, I advise you to learn all these things.

Those who learn to be diplomats must be trained to contact people. Not only must they be courteous, but they must also have a certain demeanor. A diplomat represents his country. Therefore, when he meets with the heads of other countries, he must have a proper demeanor in order to gain others' respect before he can gain their trust. We are not uplifting ourselves, but when we speak for the Lord, we are what Paul calls an ambassador of Christ (2 Cor. 5:20; Eph. 6:20). Hence, we should learn to speak and conduct ourselves with gravity even though we are young. We should not be hasty in our speaking; rather, when we speak, we should consider to whom we are speaking, what to say, how much to say, and when to stop speaking.

We must learn all these things because we represent the Lord. Suppose you are a young sister who recently graduated from college. You will know how to conduct yourself and how to speak with gravity if you are properly aggressive. The saints in your small group will be impressed and think that you are special. If the Spirit leads you, you can pray a few simple and weighty sentences. After the meeting, you will not be frivolous; rather, your contact with others will be proper before leaving. This will leave the saints in your small group with the impression that you are a person who is worthy of respect. Even your reading of the Bible should be proper in a small group. If you conduct yourself in this way, the saints in your group will be gained by your proper reading. Thus, over time you will build up a certain amount of credibility among them.

The Lord raised up a church in my hometown when I was young. A year later the Lord led me to leave my job, and after that He took me to Shanghai. At that time I prayed that the Lord would give me wisdom to know how to go out and come in among His people (cf. 2 Chron. 1:9-10). I prayed this for at least two or three years, and I believe that the Lord heard my prayer. We must be aggressive. We should pray concerning the way we dress. We should consider even the style and the color of the clothes we wear. We must not love fashion. As soon as we dress fashionably, we sell ourselves cheaply. However, we should not dress like an old person. When we pray concerning how to dress appropriately, the Lord will lead us.

You should conduct yourselves such that others consider you as weighty young persons full of gravity. If others have this impression of you, your words will have weight. People will be amazed that you are only in your twenties, and they will treasure and receive your words.

I was saved through the gospel preached by Sister Peace Wang. I was not yet twenty years old then, and she was a young woman who was six years older than I. When she preached the gospel in my hometown, I went to hear her out of curiosity. As she was speaking, I was greatly touched, and I received everything she said. I was genuinely saved at that time. Seven years later the Lord raised up a church in my hometown, and in the spring of the following year, around March or April, she was the first person who came to visit us. We observed her attitude, her mannerisms, her way of contacting people, and the way she handled things. Everything she did impressed us. At that time she was a very influential sister in Christianity. No matter what she did, whether she was standing to give a message or sitting down, she impressed others. It was not only the power in her spirit that impressed others, but much more it was her demeanor.

You must learn all these things. You should not behave in a loose or crazy way, nor should you be old fashioned or too conservative. You must pray and learn to be appropriate.

Even how we style our hair requires much learning. We must not forget that serving the Lord is contacting people, and an important part of contacting people is our appearance, because this affects the impression that others have of us. Hence, we must be aggressive to learn, even in the matter of cutting our hair.

These points illustrate that we must learn to be aggressive in everything. If the two hundred full-timers are aggressive to learn, even your hairstyle and clothing will show others your quality. All these things are related to your serving the Lord; hence, you must be aggressive, not casual, in everything.

QUESTIONS AND ANSWERS

Question: If a Christian who claims that he is Elijah, sent by Jehovah to help others, comes to our small group meeting, how should we handle him?

Answer: We should simply tell him, "We are open to all who are saved, but we will not receive such speaking. Let me escort you to the door."

Question: How can we get to know the actual situation of the people we contact?

Answer: In order to do anything, we must have the proper knowledge. If you gave me an English essay to correct, but I did not know English, I could read it a hundred times and still be unable to correct it, because I do not have the necessary knowledge. I would need sufficient knowledge of English grammar in order to correct the essay. Similarly, our ability to know people depends on two factors: how much we have learned and how much we know the spirit of others. We cannot know a person by listening merely to his words; we must touch his spirit with our spirit. How much we have learned to exercise our spirit determines our ability to know others. This cannot be learned in one day; it can only be learned over time. A person who handles fabric every day is able to tell whether a fabric is good or not simply by touching it. Whether we are able to render some help to others depends on how much we know them.

Question: Many of us grew up in the children's meetings. We love the Lord and the church, and we desire to serve Him full time. How do we conduct ourselves before the older saints who have seen us grow up?

Answer: This is a difficult point. On the one hand, a prophet has no honor in his own country (John 4:44; Matt. 13:57), but on the other hand, as your speech and mannerisms change, and you become stable and serious, the older saints will feel different about you. The most important thing is to always appropriately present yourself before people. For this reason, when you return to your locality, you must be aggressive and make progress so that others will respect you. The attitude of the saints depends on how you present yourself. This does not mean that we are pretentious or put on airs but that we are real.

Question: What do we do if a weak and backslidden brother comes to a small group meeting and expresses his negative views concerning the church?

Answer: Everything depends on the circumstance. Nevertheless, the brothers and sisters need a broad heart, and they need to be considerate of the weak saints who have not been meeting for a while. We should not be offended by what he says. However, if he does this every time, we should ask him to stop his negative speaking or to stay home. Moreover, the saints in the small group should pray, asking for the Lord's leading concerning how to help such saints. We should not be quick to address the situation. We need a broad and patient heart, and we need to follow the Lord's leading in the situation to render him some help.

Question: Eighty percent of the saints in my small group are older saints who have been in the small group for some time; it is therefore easy for them to practice the group meeting as they have in the past. What should we do to turn them to the present practice?

Answer: You should not be legal in adopting the present practice. You should not be "reformers" and attempt to change everything once you join a small group. You should simply meet with the saints. Gradually, as you gain their trust, you can begin to speak to them. Even if you make no progress for a year, there is still the next year. The Lord Jesus is full of patience toward us. With Him a thousand years are like one day (2 Pet. 3:8). Hence, we should not be anxious. Our goal is to bring the brothers and sisters to exercise their life function. Some of them might already have formed habits that are difficult to break; nevertheless, we must not cut them off. The Lord will operate and raise up some who have the same vision and burden as we do. We should believe in the Lord.

As you young people go to serve the Lord, you must avoid rushing into things. Instead, you should exercise patience. This does not mean that you should not do anything, or that you should not be concerned or positive. On the contrary, you must be positive, concerned, and burdened but at the same time realize that you must not be hasty in the situation and circumstance. The saints may not be able to match your burden; hence, you need to give the Lord some time to raise up the proper atmosphere. Then the saints will change their view and their attitude, and there will be plenty to do. This can be compared to a farmer who plants seeds and tills the ground in December. This is foolishness; his effort is in vain. Instead, he should be actively getting ready and waiting so that he will be able to plant seeds when spring arrives.

You should not be quick to do anything. You should not say, "I have participated in the training. Now I have a heavy burden to change the situation in my church." I guarantee that if you do this, you will fail. When you return, you should learn to be patient and wise. You should allow the Lord to change winter into spring in His timing. While you wait, you must pray to prepare yourself and also exercise to make progress. You should learn how to converse with the older saints. If you do not succeed, you can try another way. This is being aggressive, and this is the way to learn to serve the Lord. You need to learn in all these things.

Question: Since the success of a small group depends on whether the leading ones have a clear burden, should we have a training for the leading ones so that we may all get the help?

Answer: This training is to charge you full-timers to be aggressive to learn so that when you join a small group meeting, you will function spontaneously. If it is needed, you may follow the Lord's leading and share a little concerning His present leading in the church in relation to the small group meeting. Your purpose is not to promote the small groups or to arrange the saints into small groups. That is organization. Our desire is that you function in the Body and bring a little spark of fire with you. The church is not an organization; rather, the church is like an orchard with all kinds of trees. Some trees may not grow so well for a time, but after a while an opportunity will arise, and the timing will be right. We must continue to meet, and the Holy Spirit will lead us. We are not an organization; there is no need to have a set of regulations. We have the Lord, the Spirit, and the Word.

Question: Does the church have a plan for nurturing the brothers and sisters? How do we help the brothers and sisters become persons who are faithful and prudent?

Answer: The church life is a life of nurturing. If we meet regularly, we will be nurtured and nourished. At the same time, the church life causes every saint's gift and talent to be manifested. Hence, the church life does not suppress the saints; rather, it encourages everyone to manifest his ability so that the gifts and talents are manifested. The churches should encourage the brothers and sisters to travel abroad to visit other countries. This is beneficial. However, we do not wish to make such things into rules, because the church is the Lord's organic Body; everything in the church depends on life.

ABOUT THE AUTHOR

Witness Lee was born in 1905 in northern China and raised in a Christian family. At age 19 he was fully captured for Christ and immediately consecrated himself to preach the gospel for the rest of his life. Early in his service, he met Watchman Nee, a renowned preacher, teacher, and writer. Witness Lee labored together with Watchman Nee under his direction. In 1934 Watchman Nee entrusted Witness Lee with the responsibility for his publication operation, called the Shanghai Gospel Bookroom.

Prior to the Communist takeover in 1949, Witness Lee was sent by Watchman Nee and his other co-workers to Taiwan to ensure that the things delivered to them by the Lord would not be lost. Watchman Nee instructed Witness Lee to continue the former's publishing operation abroad as the Taiwan Gospel Bookroom, which has been publicly recognized as the publisher of Watchman Nee's works outside China. Witness Lee's work in Taiwan manifested the Lord's abundant blessing. From a mere 350 believers, newly fled from the mainland, the churches in Taiwan grew to 20,000 in five years.

In 1962 Witness Lee felt led of the Lord to come to the United States, and he began to minister in Los Angeles. During his 35 years of service in the U.S., he ministered in weekly meetings and weekend conferences, delivering several thousand spoken messages. Much of his speaking has since been published as over 400 titles. Many of these have been translated into over fourteen languages. He gave his last public conference in February 1997 at the age of 91.

He leaves behind a prolific presentation of the truth in the Bible. His major work, *Life-study of the Bible,* comprises over 25,000 pages of commentary on every book of the Bible from the perspective of the believers' enjoyment and experience of God's divine life in Christ through the Holy Spirit. Witness Lee was the chief editor of a new translation of the New Testament into Chinese called the Recovery Version and directed the translation of the same into English. The Recovery Version also appears in a number of other languages. He provided an extensive body of footnotes, outlines, and spiritual cross references. A radio broadcast of his messages can be heard on Christian radio stations in the United States. In 1965 Witness Lee founded Living Stream Ministry, a non-profit corporation, located in Anaheim, California, which officially presents his and Watchman Nee's ministry.

Witness Lee's ministry emphasizes the experience of Christ as life and the practical oneness of the believers as the Body of Christ. Stressing the importance of attending to both these matters, he led the churches under his care to grow in Christian life and function. He was unbending in his conviction that God's goal is not narrow sectarianism but the Body of Christ. In time, believers began to meet simply as the church in their localities in response to this conviction. In recent years a number of new churches have been raised up in Russia and in many European countries.

OTHER BOOKS PUBLISHED BY
Living Stream Ministry

Titles by Witness Lee:

Abraham—Called by God	978-0-7363-0359-0
The Experience of Life	978-0-87083-417-2
The Knowledge of Life	978-0-87083-419-6
The Tree of Life	978-0-87083-300-7
The Economy of God	978-0-87083-415-8
The Divine Economy	978-0-87083-268-0
God's New Testament Economy	978-0-87083-199-7
The World Situation and God's Move	978-0-87083-092-1
Christ vs. Religion	978-0-87083-010-5
The All-inclusive Christ	978-0-87083-020-4
Gospel Outlines	978-0-87083-039-6
Character	978-0-87083-322-9
The Secret of Experiencing Christ	978-0-87083-227-7
The Life and Way for the Practice of the Church Life	978-0-87083-785-2
The Basic Revelation in the Holy Scriptures	978-0-87083-105-8
The Crucial Revelation of Life in the Scriptures	978-0-87083-372-4
The Spirit with Our Spirit	978-0-87083-798-2
Christ as the Reality	978-0-87083-047-1
The Central Line of the Divine Revelation	978-0-87083-960-3
The Full Knowledge of the Word of God	978-0-87083-289-5
Watchman Nee—A Seer of the Divine Revelation ...	978-0-87083-625-1

Titles by Watchman Nee:

How to Study the Bible	978-0-7363-0407-8
God's Overcomers	978-0-7363-0433-7
The New Covenant	978-0-7363-0088-9
The Spiritual Man • 3 volumes	978-0-7363-0269-2
Authority and Submission	978-0-7363-0185-5
The Overcoming Life	978-1-57593-817-2
The Glorious Church	978-0-87083-745-6
The Prayer Ministry of the Church	978-0-87083-860-6
The Breaking of the Outer Man and the Release ...	978-1-57593-955-1
The Mystery of Christ	978-1-57593-954-4
The God of Abraham, Isaac, and Jacob	978-0-87083-932-0
The Song of Songs	978-0-87083-872-9
The Gospel of God • 2 volumes	978-1-57593-953-7
The Normal Christian Church Life	978-0-87083-027-3
The Character of the Lord's Worker	978-1-57593-322-1
The Normal Christian Faith	978-0-87083-748-7
Watchman Nee's Testimony	978-0-87083-051-8

Available at
Christian bookstores, or contact Living Stream Ministry
2431 W. La Palma Ave. • Anaheim, CA 92801
1-800-549-5164 • www.livingstream.com